AF342157

BICYCLING 1874
A Textbook for Early Riders

BICYCLING

1874

A Textbook for Early Riders

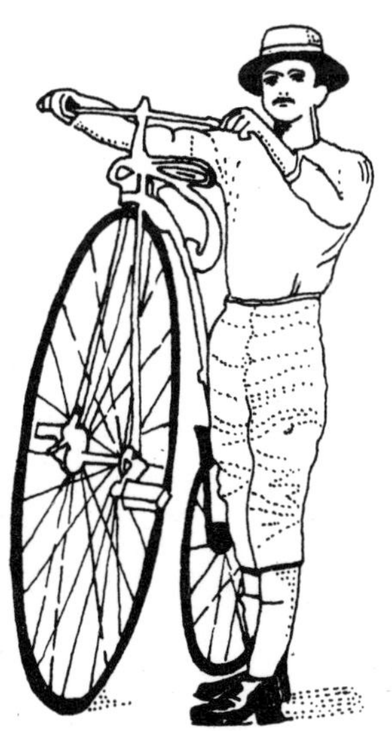

DAVID & CHARLES REPRINTS

TAPLINGER PUBLISHING COMPANY

This reprint of a handbook first published in London in 1874 shows how rapidly the bicycle became a tool for social and economic change, as cyclists blazed a trail on many British and European roads that then carried virtually no through traffic but which were to become main tourist arteries in the motor era.

This impression first published in Great Britain in 1970 by
DAVID & CHARLES (PUBLISHERS) LIMITED
Newton Abbot Devon
and in the United States of America by
TAPLINGER PUBLISHING CO., INC.
New York
British ISBN 0 7153 4934 1
American ISBN 0-8008-0738-3
Library of Congress Catalog Number 76-123436 (Taplinger)

Printed in Great Britain by
Latimer Trend & Company Limited Whitstable

BICYCLING:

ITS RISE AND DEVELOPMENT,

A TEXT BOOK FOR RIDERS.

WITH NUMEROUS ILLUSTRATIONS.

" Go, little book, God send thee good passage,
And specially let this be thy prayere,
Unto them all that thee will read or hear,
Where thou art wrong, after their help to call,
Thee to correct in any part or all."—CHAUCER.

" Vires acquirit eundo."

LONDON:

TINSLEY BROS., 8, CATHERINE STREET, STRAND.

1874.

PREFACE.

We have desired in the compilation of this volume to supply, in an attractive form, an admitted want. During the existence of the wooden-wheel velocipedes, and when, in 1869-70, those vehicles showed some signs of vitality, several books appeared on the subject. When wooden-wheel machines went out of use, these books became valueless, and now not half-a-dozen lines in any of them would be found applicable to the Bicycle of to-day, and not a word in them would be of the least instruction to the Bicyclist. During the last three years the Bicycle movement has rapidly advanced in public favour, and there seems to be little doubt that the practical utility of these machines will lead to their speedy adoption for many purposes of business, or pleasure. The newspapers have fully recognised the importance of the movement, and duly record the achievements of its votaries. Ten thousand persons have assembled at one time to witness a Bicycle contest, and the best manufacturers are in arrears with their orders for machines. In the face of these facts, it must appear strange that there should not be in existence a single book of reference, or guidance on this subject, We have, therefore, ventured to supply the want with a brief volume, which will, we trust, be found practical, trustworthy, and instructive.

The records of matches and feats are sufficiently full to furnish material for a history of Bicycling; the illustrations are numerous, and are especially intended to assist beginners; the instructions are simple and practical; the list of Clubs is a new feature; and we hope the sketches of Tours at home and abroad will be found useful to those who may have the good fortune to enjoy from time to time a few days' holiday.

In conclusion, we would add that we shall always be obliged by the communication of any interesting information about Bicycling for adoption in future editions.

THE EDITOR,

LONDON, *December 1874.*

CONTENTS.

INDEX TO ROUTES.

ENGLAND.

SCOTLAND.

SWITZERLAND.

BELGIUM.

FRANCE.

ENGLAND.

ENGLAND—(continued).

IRELAND.

SCOTLAND.

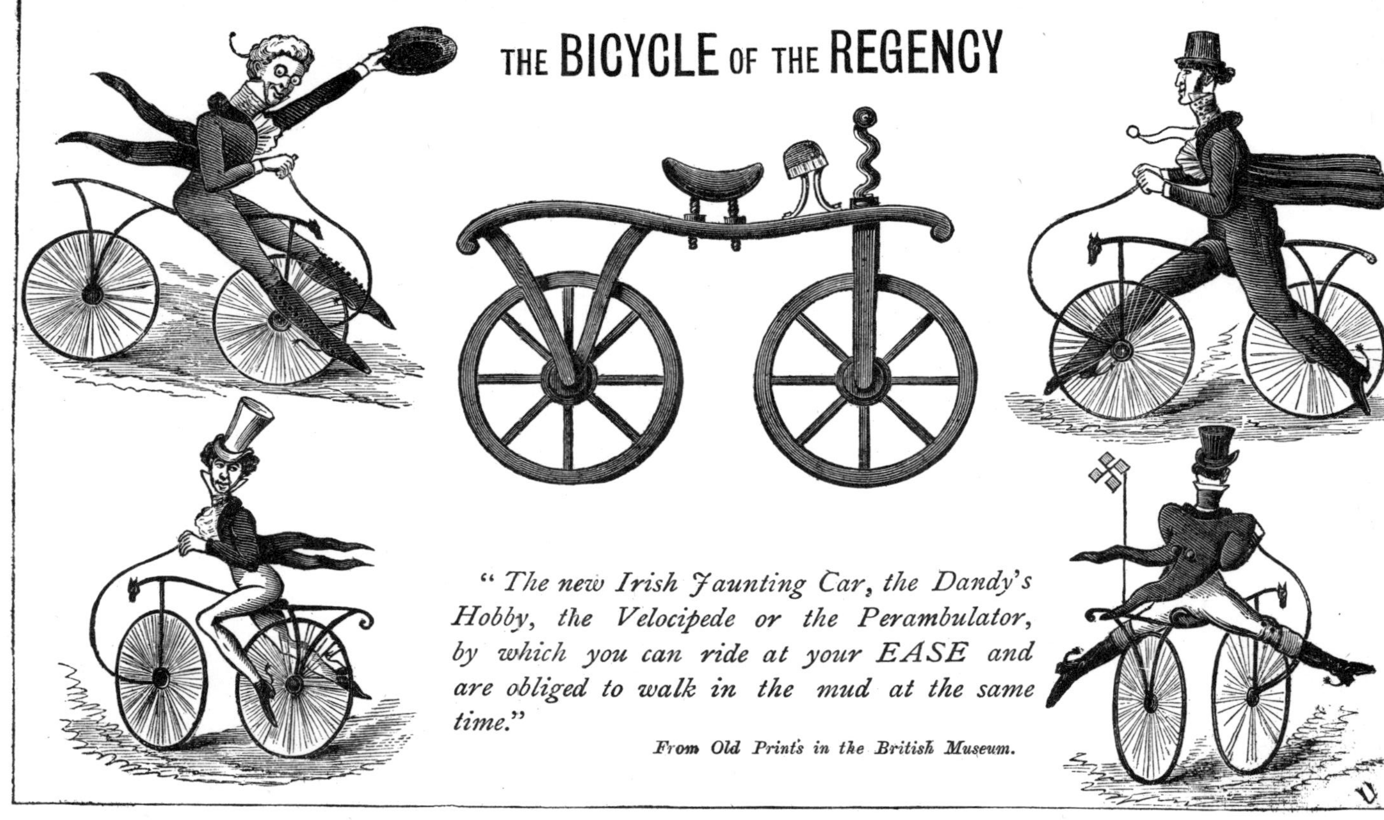

THE BICYCLE OF THE REGENCY

" The new Irish Jaunting Car, the Dandy's Hobby, the Velocipede or the Perambulator, by which you can ride at your EASE and are obliged to walk in the mud at the same time."

From Old Prints in the British Museum.

CHAPTER I.

The Birth of the Bicycle.

HAT neither the means, nor the skill "to witch the world with noble horsemanship" has been granted to all, or to even most of us, is a mere truism. We were taught in our Mavor's Spelling to accept the fact that, " the horse is a noble animal and very useful to man;" but it was with a mental reservation, as the latter part of the axiom is not universally true. We had roads to travel on, too, and not seeing our way to pressing into our locomotive service, like other less favoured nations, elephants, camels, reindeer, or ostriches, it required but little time to arrive at the conclusion that wheels were necessary to supplement the services of that popular institution vulgarly known as "shanks' pony"; and velocipedes of many wheels appeared, some as far back as the close of the eighteenth century. We do not propose to dwell on the polycycle, as we may call it. It had three, four, five, or six wheels in the various stages of its existence, and carried two or more persons sitting side by side, one behind the other, or even back to back.

The year 1818 has the credit of welcoming the *début* of the father of all bicycles, which furnished the caricaturists of that era with abundant matter for the exercise of their art, the veteran George Cruikshank, amongst many others of infinitely smaller ability, extracting all the satirical fun possible out of the new invention, which came originally from Paris; was, we believe, published, so to speak, in London, and was jointly *exploitée* by Mr. Johnson, a coach maker of Long Acre, and a certain Baron von Brais. It had been patented in Paris, and soon appeared in London, doubtless with all the " latest improvements!" The popularity it enjoyed for a few years was probably due to the fact that London has a distinctly characteristic habit of adopting Parisian novelties with inexplicable avidity, simply because they are Parisian. The costume of 1818 was hardly adapted to the use of this early bicycle, so that the merciless caricaturists* of the " Dandy," or " Hobby Horse," as it was indifferently called, easily conjured up all sorts of fantastic exaggerations of the appearance of its riders, and that "ridicule," which the French proverb says, " kills," did its deadly work on the senior member of the bicycle family, and there was an end of it. It was as well that it was so; the affair was a thing "fearfully and wonderfully made," and consisted of a pair of wooden wheels of equal diameter, braced to-

gether tandem-fashion, betwixt which, on a wooden bar, the rider sat, impelling the
" horse " by thrusting the ground with his feet.   Whether velocity, comfort, or
elegance were derivable from this piece of Long Acre, or Rue St. Denis
ingenuity, we may perhaps be permitted to doubt.   Some of its admirers claimed
a speed of about ten miles an hour for it, a sheer impossibility, even when going
down a steep incline.   The weight of the bulky wooden machine, the friction of
its bearings, and the slight motive power being taken into consideration, its
progress along a level road could not have greatly exceeded the pace of a rapid
pedestrian.   Thus the first bicycle failed, although an attempt to utilize it for the
French postmen had been made.   Nobody regretted its extinction, except
perhaps the boot makers, and Mr. Johnson of Long Acre.

The application of direct pedal power to the driving wheel appeared next,
and was hampered by an intricate arrangement of levers, toothed racks, cogs and
pinions (the friction of which neutralized what little force was obtainable by
pedal labour), or in some cases by the driver's feet and hands together.   English,
French, American, and German inventors appear to have been alike disheartened
at the difficulties they had to encounter ; and although many patents were taken
out between 1818 and 1831, the records of the Patent Office evidence neither
real progress, nor ingenuity on the part of bicycle or velocipede makers until about
twelve years ago.   Public attention had not to any notable extent been drawn
hitherto to the inventions that had appeared ; the impression prevailed that this
kind of riding was a hobby of a puerile kind, and that its utility during its career
was about equal to that of the Sedan chair with no bottom, in which the Irishman
rode, remarking at the end of his journey that, he thought " he might as well have
walked if it hadn't been for the look of the thing."   Moreover, the ridicule the
old dandy horse elicited had not been lived down.   However, in 1862 an
awakening took place ; the simplicity of a crank action on a rotating axle
appeared to have its charms for inventors of all nations, and our American
cousins came to the front at once, the running being made for them by a
Frenchman who just missed giving the world a bicycle almost identical with
that now so familiar to us.

THE BICYCLE OF 1869.

Thenceforward the development of the bicycle has been steadily, if not very rapidly, progressing. M. Michaux of Paris has the credit of enlarging the driving wheel, and his machines were popularized in this country several years ago. Unfortunately, however, for the growth of bicycle riding, the principal patrons of the vehicle were of the hobbledehoy class, whose Sunday performances were dangerous to themselves and every one else. Respectable people did not take to them kindly until M. Magee (also dating from Paris) discarded wood altogether in the construction of his two wheeled velocipedes, in favour of iron and steel, and lightened the vehicle until it assumed a more elegant appearance than it had ever previously attained. At last it began to be admitted that bicycling had "something in it"—there were enhanced velocity and many other advantages discoverable in the new French Machine, and some very respectable journeys both as to time and distance were accomplished. It remained, however, for our own countrymen to supplement M. Magee's invention, and this the Coventry Machinists' Company did, by the introduction of more and more improvements until they were enabled to produce a bicycle as superior to those then in existence as the first crank action machine was to the hobby horse of the Regency. They

THE BICYCLE OF 1874.

introduced the now almost universally adopted "spider" wheel, with rubber tyres and step, diminished the size of the hind wheel, enlarged the forewheel to an extent that no previous riders or makers ever dreamed possible, and produced a bicycle combining with extreme lightness all the advantages of elegance, noiselessness and immense speed. The new Roadster Machine weighs only some forty to fifty pounds as against eighty to a hundred under the old conditions of manufacture. A modern Racing Bicycle, with a frontwheel sixty inches in diameter, weighs something under fifty pounds. Thus a safe, practical and useful bicycle was made an accomplished fact, and from that moment its success was assured. The arrangements of springs, brakes and rubber tyres, have removed half the terrors of ruts and steep gradients, and the testimony of hundreds of experienced bicyclists is that a bicycle is more useful than the cleverest nag man ever bestrode, with the additional advantage that a bicycle consumes nothing but a little oil.

The price of a high-class bicycle will be found to vary from 11 guineas to 16 guineas, according to the diameter of the wheel, the quality being precisely the same.

Prejudices are being rapidly removed; confidence in the utility of the bicycle is becoming stronger day by day; and in a future chapter we shall briefly allude to some of the remarkable results already achieved by skilled bicyclists. We do not know whether Mr. Henry Ward Beecher's announcement from the pulpit, "that he was about to become a bicyclist, and that his congregation would, "an' they loved him," follow suit, &c., "and flock to his conventicle on myriads of velocipedes," has resulted in fulfilment, but we do know that a greater man than he, the late Professor Faraday, constructed, as well as rode, some sort of velocipede, which would certainly have been a bicycle had he lived in the days of the " Coventry Spiders "; and a late Cabinet Minister is known to have become a most efficient rider.

The *Graphic* * is responsible for the following—"A tricycle society is now in course of formation, and ladies are especially invited to become members. There is no indelicacy, say the promoters, in a lady using one. One gentleman and his wife " did " North Wales last summer, he taking the luggage and she the baby, and their pace was from eight to ten miles an hour." There must be a considerable improvement upon the existing methods of constructing tricycles before there can be any hope of success for them. Cumbersome and clumsy as they now are, a speed of eight or ten miles an hour could only be attained by such an expenditure of manual and pedal labour as to make one shudder at the thought of doing anything like a distance in hot summer weather. But in machines where there is so much room for improvement, improvements would be sure to spring up, if any serious demand were created for them.

As bicycling has a history of its own, so has it its literature and its slang. From the far west we learn that the various stages of bicyclical ability are ticketed thus,—the tyros are " timid toddlers," progression is marked by the stages of " wary wobblers" and "go it gracefuls," and to those who achieve the acme of perfection is accorded the proud title of the " fancy few."

* *September 16th 1874.*

CHAPTER II.

Riding and Learning to Ride.

"AN OUNCE of knowledge is worth a ton of theory," and there is no royal road to bicycle riding any more than there is to the attainment of any other desirable object. Cases are on record of persons learning the art in an incredibly short space of time, and we were informed the other day of an instance of a rider who purchased a machine at a large provincial factory, and after being shown simply how to mount, actually rode away on it, without any previous practice. Such instances are however extremely rare, and must not be allowed to mislead. Patient persevering practice is required to become a proficient and elegant bicyclist.

In the choice of a bicycle it is undoubtedly the truest economy to purchase only the best quality, and that from a well-known manufacturer, whose reputation is the buyer's best safeguard for the superiority of the machines he sells.

For if it be considered that a bicycle, which must bear the wear and tear of all kinds of roads, and carry a weight of ten to fourteen stone at a rate of twelve to fifteen miles an hour, for days together if necessary, weighs only forty-five pounds, it will be at once conceded that not only must it be made of the very best materials which money can buy, but that its construction demands also the finest mechanical skill and ability which can be bestowed upon it.

Second rate material, and second rate labour, are not only absolutely unreliable, but perilous to life and limb. This warning cannot be too strenuously enforced.

A high class bicycle is not expensive beyond the first outlay; it may be ridden daily, and will last for years if only ordinary attention be paid to keeping the wearing parts well cleaned and lubricated with the best sperm oil.* Even should a casualty occur, in most cases the necessary repairs and adjustments can be done at a trifling cost.

By way of illustration, we heard the other day of an overthrown bicycle being run over by a dray, at Aldershot, all the wheels of which passed over

See Page 11.

it; **nevertheless the rider** was able to proceed after a few adjustments had been made.   Another bicycle was run-down by a van belonging to a menagerie, and although the wheel was knocked into the shape of a badly executed figure of 8, no single spoke, screw, spring, or bearing was broken, and in a few hours the machine was made as efficient as before.   These were high-class bicycles. On the other hand, you may, during the season, read almost weekly, in the *Field*, of tourists whose journeys have been delayed, or altogether abandoned, through such mishaps as " broken backbones," " broken spokes," and we have even seen " broken tyres."   And to such reports you see almost invariably attached the name of a second-class maker.

The best known makers are Sparrow, of London, Keen, of Surbiton, Timberlake, of Maidenhead, Humber, of Nottingham, and The Coventry Machinists' Company, of Coventry; the latter are the oldest established and by far the largest makers in the country, if indeed their factory and plant be not the largest in the world for the manufacture of bicycles.

It is well for the beginner not to be too ambitious about the size of the driving-wheel; confidence is more certainly acquirable on a small wheel, although that is pretty certain to be soon discarded for the largest possible radius the rider's length of leg can compass, for the sake of the speed thereby to be obtained without any greater labour.

Where practicable, it is very advisable to learn on a small wooden machine, and we say, *experto crede*, this will not be injured in appearance by the few harmless falls that the tyro generally has to take in the beginning, with the best grace he may.   Decidedly the better way in the first instance is to obtain the assistance of a friend, and this there can be little difficulty in doing.   The knack of

BALANCING

is really all there is to be actually *learned*, the rest comes by practice, and that gives the confidence which enables riders to do the great things in the way of speed and distance that the equestrian may sigh for in vain.

FRIENDLY HELP.　　　　　　　　　　　A GENTLE PUSH.

On *a gentle slope* and on a machine with a small wheel, you may then, alone if necessary, take your seat, and proceed, grasping the handle, not too tightly, but

NEVER LEANING ON IT,

and if your machine be low enough for your feet to just touch the ground, so much the better. If you find the balance difficult to acquire on starting, and that the machine has an inclination to fall, a mere touch with the toe, on the ground, on whichever side the machine is falling, will right you again. The *pedals* MUST NOT BE USED in the first essays, the impetus given by the incline being sufficient to move the machine with quite enough velocity for you to learn to balance and steer. When you have mastered this, you have learned all that a bicyclist needs by way of precept. The next thing is to accustom the feet and legs to the motion of the pedals, in order to do which, it is necessary to place the feet lightly on them, allowing the motion of the machine to carry them round. Do not attempt to exert any pressure on the pedals until you become thoroughly accustomed to their motion. As your feet are now employed and cannot touch the ground to restore equilibrium, if you experience a tendency to fall, bear in mind,

TO TURN THE WHEEL GENTLY AND WITHOUT THE SLIGHTEST JERK IN THE
DIRECTION THE BICYCLE IS FALLING.

This is the whole secret of success in bicycle riding, and cannot be too attentively observed. To a finished rider this motion is an instinct, but, until you arrive at this stage of perfection, it will need to be carefully remembered and practised. *If you turn the wheel in the opposite direction you will assuredly fall.* We have heard many people say, "Why! I should have turned the wheel just the opposite way!" but we repeat this is an error, it *must* be turned in the direction in which you have a tendency to fall, and the more skilfully you bring the rule into practice, the more certain and speedy will be your progress. After a little experience in riding, so that you have become somewhat accustomed to the balance and the pedals, you may endeavour to MOUNT. This, it is advisable, should be first attempted from some support, such as a wall or post, and NOT *by the step.* You will by this means gradually acquire the confidence necessary to mount and also dismount by means of the step in the proper manner. To mount by a wall you place the machine in a nearly upright position against it, placing the pedal, that is away from the wall, just past the top of the throw. This

A FRIENDLY WALL.

is to ensure your getting a good start with your outside foot. Mount your machine and take hold of the outside handle, but with the other hand steady yourself against the wall, gently bringing the machine into a perpendicular position. As soon as it has attained this, push your outside pedal downwards, this will give you the requisite start and enable you to bring your other foot into use. This way of mounting will answer your purpose until you have

MOUNTING.

arrived at some proficiency as a rider; you may then endeavour to do so in the ordinary way, by means of the step. To do this, take the machine by both handles, place the left toe upon the step, and, taking two or three short hops to get a little "way" on the machine, raise yourself on the step and drop into the saddle. In learning, it is always best to do this on a gentle descent; it is also desirable, *in order to avoid a fall, to keep the wheel turned about two inches out of the perpendicular and* TOWARDS YOU, so that, in the event of your not succeeding in reaching the saddle at the first attempt, you will drop on the side you started from.

It is quite impossible to state arbitrarily how long this state of pupilage will last. No two riders, on comparing notes, ever find their experiences coincident. We can only counsel patience and resolution, and give the assurance that bicycling is not so difficult after all, and that success is within easy reach of all who persevere; a few hours being generally enough to learn each successive stage on the way to complete mastery over the machine. Frequent practice *(but not by exhaustive spells of work)* is of the greatest importance; and a sure aid to the maintenance of self-possession is to bear continually in mind the few precepts

FALLING.

we venture to give. Of course, an impending fall, if not checked by gently and slightly turning the front wheel in the direction you are falling, as previously suggested,—must be submitted to, and rendered as little unpleasant as possible; we therefore counsel the rider to yield to the machine if it does not immediately right itself on the action of the handle, and waiting till it has nearly reached the ground, then throw out the leg. The acquisition of a graceful and easy seat, and the economy of your motive power are the next two things to be striven for. Avoid stiffness, whether in the joints of the legs and arms, or in the pose of the body, and do not attempt to sit rigidly upright with military exactness. The act of dismounting being exactly the converse of mounting, it is scarcely necessary to say more than that the left toe should be accustomed to seek the step and find it with ease, whereupon the rider can drop lightly on the ground on his right foot, not relinquishing his hold of the machine handle until he is safe on terra firma. Experienced riders generally acquire the habit of descending without using the step, and leave the machine from the treadle direct, or by throwing the left leg over the handle. A tyro should never attempt this.

THE LEG-REST—DOWN-HILL.

DISMOUNTING.

The use of the leg-rest is shown in the accompanying cut. The rider, on descending hills, can rest from the labour of working the treadles, and merely steer his course with the handle.

Acrobatic performances, such as riding side-saddle fashion and standing on the seat like a circus-rider, are occasionally to be seen. The learner should never attempt anything of the sort until his mastery over the machine is quite perfect, even then he will do well to avoid these displays, and give his attention to the increase of his speed of travelling.

PRACTICE MAKES PERFECT.

Bicycling has many advantages for all classes : in addition to its acknowledged utility to country clergymen and doctors, road surveyors, and others who have long rounds to perform, and who are so rapidly adopting the machines, we are glad to add the testimony of a very hard-worked body of men, the letter-carriers, who, with this aid to locomotion, can perform their "weary round" of ten or twenty miles with scarcely any fatigue. The healthiness of the exercise has never been questioned; the difficulties of learning are not greater than those of horse-riding, skating, or swimming, and the acquisition places a man of ordinary strength in a position equal,—nay, superior to— the trained professional jockey, or pedestrian, inasmuch as he has his motive power contained within himself, and that power is augmented, as well as economized, by the improved mechanism of the bicycle of to-day. If bicycling continues to increase in popularity as it is increasing, Mr. Disraeli's lament last session, that, "the British race is in a state of physical decline," may well be withdrawn. There is no exercise so salutary for the development of the muscles of arms, legs, and back, and the bicyclists may well take for their own the trite motto,

THE RACING BICYCLE OF 1874.

Directions for Oiling Bicycles and keeping them in order.

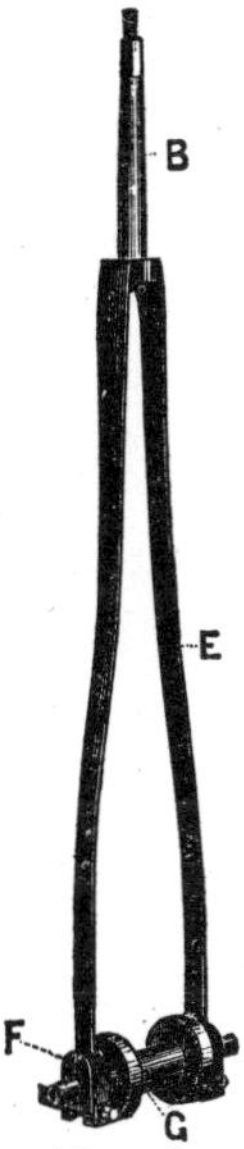

Keep the bearings well oiled with the best Sperm oil, not using too much at one time, but putting in a little before each ride, or if on a long journey a little may be added with advantage while you are on the road.

The oilholes for front bearings are on the outside of the Fork Ends F. (fig. 1), while the Back Wheel is oiled by removing the screw M. (fig. 4.) In each of the front bearings is a piece of sponge, in a recess cut for the purpose underneath the oil holes. Care must be taken when it may be necessary to take out the Front Wheel, that the sponges do not drop out and are lost ; they should occasionally be taken out and cleaned, as they serve the very important purpose of keeping away from the wheel spindle, and bearings, any grit that may get into the oil holes.

There are two other parts which require occasional oiling, viz :—the Socket and Treadles. At the top of the Socket A (fig. 2), is a small hole. which is the outlet of a Spiral Groove running round the spindle inside the Socket; into this hole the oil should be poured, but, like the wheels, it is better with only a small quantity at a time. On each of the Treadles is a Brass Cap, which must be unscrewed to admit the oil being poured in, and the machine should be inclined well over, so as to allow of the oil running well in—even when in constant use once or twice a week is ample for lubricating the Treadles.

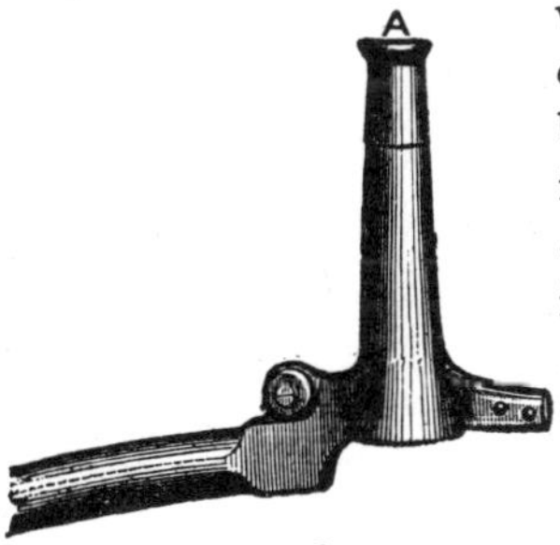

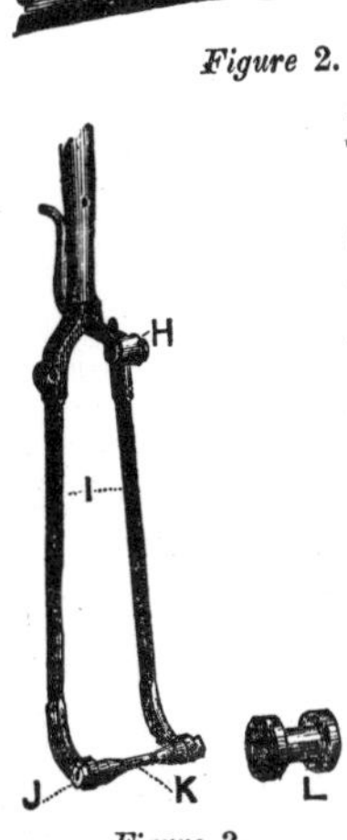

Figure 1.

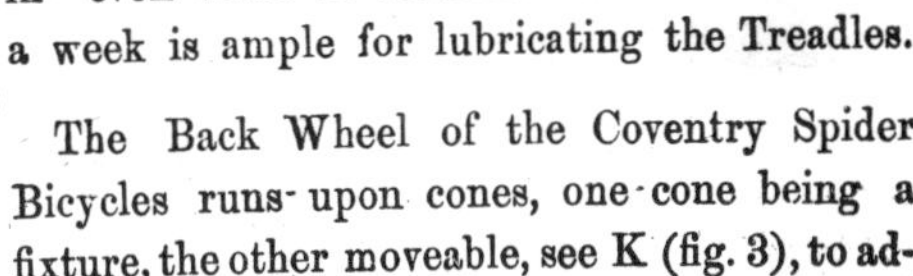

Figure 2.

The Back Wheel of the Coventry Spider Bicycles runs upon cones, one cone being a fixture, the other moveable, see K (fig. 3), to adjust which it is necessary to slacken the nut J (fig. 3), then draw the end of the Fork out a short distance and turn the moveable cone round by means of the two small flat faces on the end of it, so as to prevent all side-shake, *but not to jam the wheel*, then screw the nut up tightly ; care is needed not to reverse the pin, when at any time the wheel is taken out for cleaning.

In illustration 3, H is the Brake—I is the Back Fork—J is the set Nut—K is the Cones and Pin—L is the Back Wheel Hub.

In illustration 4, M is the Thumb-Screw.

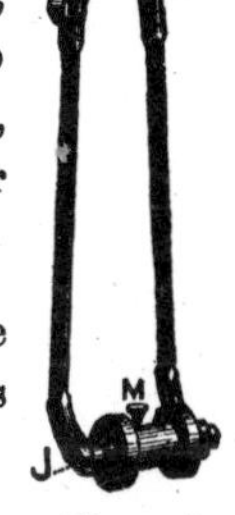

Figure 3.

Figure 4.

CHAPTER III.

Records of Bicycling.

RANTED that the old proverb, "Emulation is the Mother of Excellence," be true in any case, certainly it is so in that of bicycling. Each man wants to excel his neighbour, and each bicyclist wishes to surpass his fellow, either in speed or elegance, or both ; hence racing. And *àpropos* of racing, what a vast improvement on the ancient chariots would the bicycle have been had any of the ancient Greeks had *νους* enough to invent one ! Achilles might have made better time round the walls of Ilium, even when handicapped with the dead body of Hector, had he performed on a bicycle instead of the chariot of the period. As he had not one, he was forced to go through, as best he could, his sensational and ghastly "trick-act" so minutely recorded by Homer.

It was not long after the invention of the velocipede that races were instituted, and cumbrous as were the first machines, yet velocipedists still managed to get good sport out of them.

With the bicycle, however, a new era set in, both in the machines themselves, and the pace they travelled at. The great stumbling-block in the way of the bicyclist has been, and is, the badness of our country roads ; although much has lately been done to adapt the machines to them. But still, a fair rider can tire out a good horse in a day, and a first-class performer on a saddle in an hour ; nay, more, it wants but a very middling bicyclist to keep up for a week at a pace, which would wear down the strongest and fleetest horse. It has been recently a frequent *tour de force* for good riders to " wait upon " the daily four in-hands as they leave London, and beat them in a fair race, say to·Guildford, with little difficulty, just as four men of the Coventry Club beat the Prince of Wales' carriage and four, on November 7th, from Meridan into Coventry, a distance of five miles.

One hundred miles a-day is no extraordinary feat, and has been frequently accomplished, not for one day only, but for several consecutively, and that, too, with far less fatigue than an ordinary pedestrian would experience in getting over a quarter of the distance. These statements appear startling, but a perusal of many of the trips which have been accomplished, and which will be found fully set forth in these pages, will completely substantiate their accuracy. One of the most celebrated races on record, with the exception of Mr. Stanton's recent performances, (to which we shall presently refer) is the

OXFORD AND CAMBRIDGE INTER-UNIVERSITY RACE,

run from the haunts of the Dark Blues to those of the Light Blues. The idea of the race originated at Cambridge, although that seat of learning was behind her sister in acclimatising the art of bicycling. A challenge was sent to Oxford and at once accepted, the question as to distance being left for after consideration. A considerable amount of correspondence was exchanged, and it was at length determined that the course should be from Oxford to Cambridge, through Thame, Aylesbury, Dunstable, Hitchin and Royston, and that the day of the race should be Thursday, June 18th, 1874. The competitors selected were as follows :—Oxford : Messrs. Penrose, Read, and Wing; Cambridge : Messrs. Mildmay, James, and the Hon. J. W. Plunkett. A strong north-west wind was blowing when the competitors came to the post, and at 9.30 a.m. the word to go was given. The first town reached was Thame, one hour and a quarter after the start ; the order of arriving being :—Plunkett, Mildmay, James, Wing, Penrose, and Reed. From Thame to Aylesbury the sestette went on, and thence to Leighton Buzzard, where Plunkett (who had previously met with a slight accident before reaching the first stage) stopped, thinking there was only an Oxford and a Cambridge man in front, but there James passed him. Starting again, Plunkett came up with James of Cambridge, and Wing of Oxford, at Dunstable, where Wing stopped. Plunkett, however, went on, coming up with Penrose, who had selected some shorter route, Mildmay and Reed being still a mile or so in advance. The only men now in the race were Mildmay, Reed, Plunkett, and Penrose. The next town was Hitchin, about fifteen miles from Dunstable, where Reed fell and broke his bicycle. At Hitchin the contest was virtually over, James of Cambridge, and Reed and Wing of Oxford, having given up. Finding this was the case, Plunkett stopped for eighteen minutes until Penrose came up, thence he went on to Royston, through which place Mildmay passed three-quarters of an hour previously. At the finish at Cambridge, there was naturally great excitement, the road for nearly three miles being lined with passengers and vehicles. At a quarter to seven Mildmay reached Trumpington, whence he put on a spurt for the last two miles, but two men of either University being required to win, it was doubtful how the match would go after all. In about three-quarters of an hour Mr. Plunkett appeared and passed the post, thus winning for Cambridge the first Inter-University match. This, one of the most celebrated amateur matches that has ever yet been ridden, was, we hope, only the forerunner of similar trials of skill and endurance. The time made by the winner in 84 miles, was 8 hrs. 5 m., including stoppages.

Next in point of interest is the ride from

LONDON TO JOHN O'GROAT'S.

The " Daily Telegraph" says, " The indefatigable bicycle riders who started from London on Monday, reached John o'Groat's in safety. A more extraordinary journey, prepared under more extraordinary conditions, has been seldom recorded, and a mere passing notice hardly does it justice. A distance of 800 miles has been covered in 14 days, at a rate of 60 miles a day. * * * To say that the work would tire a horse is a feeble description of it. The strongest horse would break down under such a journey, continued as it was, in successive days. Before you had got half way to the end of the journey, the Royal Humane Society would be down upon you. There is no society to prevent a man from overtasking his own strength ; cruelty to animals does not include the cruelty which man voluntarily inflicts upon himself ; so the Middlesex bicyclers dashed on their mad career unchecked, for the love of the thing, mixed, probably with a dash of the heroism that likes to be talked about as doing something which nobody did before. It is the same spirit of adventure which leads Englishmen to climb the highest peaks of Alps every autumn—the higher the peaks the better; the more dangerous the glaciers and crevasses, the better. After all, the trip to the extreme north may be as sensible as mountain climbing, though it certainly wants the hardihood and the accompaniments of glorious scenery and of mountain air almost as exhilarating as champagne.

" On the other hand, bicycle riding at the rate of 60 miles a day must have a fascination of its own. You command the most varied scenes. From town to country, from country back to town, you skim along freely, easily, quickly. You are not dependent upon coach, rail, or steamer. No horrid nightmare haunts you in bed of early trains to be caught, hurried breakfasts to be eaten, and possible mishaps in waking and in starting. You are a self-contained man, with all your resources under your own control. You are your own coachman, and your coach is probably all night in your bed room, sure not to start until it pleases you to mount and start it. * * * As an example of what a bicycle enables a man to do, upon a stretch, the bare fact of a journey so made is full of interest."

On Whit-Monday, June 2nd, 1873, at 7.30 a.m., the following gentlemen, members of the Middlesex Bicycle Club, started from Knightsbridge for their long and perilous ride to John o'Groats, on bicycles built by the well-known T. SPARROW.

Mr. Charles Leaver	- -	45-inch wheel.
Mr. Geo. Hunt	- - -	45-inch wheel.
Mr. Chas. Spencer	- -	48-inch wheel.
Mr. Wm. Wood	- -	52-inch wheel.

They arrived at Buckdean, a distance of 64 miles the same night, where they slept. The riders were opposed by a strong head wind. The roads were shockingly bad; what with the rain and the thunderstorm, the mud clogged about the wheels, which had to drive a path through the slime, and altogether the journey was performed under the greatest possible disadvantages, so that the members of the Club deserve all the more credit for the progress they have made whilst labouring under such difficulties. On Tuesday evening, Newark was reached, a distance of 127 miles from London; and on Wednesday evening the party arrived at Wentbridge, a distance of 175. The company was overtaken by a thunderstorm which greatly retarded their advance. On arriving in Yorkshire the members found the roads worse, and said that these roads were composed of a few pieces of stone and a deep stratum of creamy limestone and mud, very awkward to travel upon. On Thursday morning the party started at 10 o'clock for Witherby. The object of the journey was to put the bicycle to a really practical use, and demonstrate that it was possible for a man to go with one of these machines from one end of the United Kingdom to the other without its needing repair or breaking down on the road, despite the obstacles and difficulties met with on the journey. On Friday they reached Darlington, and an easy day's ride on Saturday brought them to Newcastle. The following Monday they ran the whole distance from Newcastle to Dunbar, whence, with due stoppages, they proceeded viâ Edinburgh and Queensferry, to Dunkeld. This latter place was left on the morning of the second Thursday, and before night they had accomplished the long and difficult journey up Garryside, and past Dalwhinnie to Kingussie—a distance of over 65 miles. Next day was pouring with rain, and the travellers were not able to make further than Moy, 20 miles south of Inverness; on Saturday they ran to Dingwall, and on Sunday proceeded to Helmsdale. They passed Brorr at eight o'clock on Sunday night at full speed, when two of them came to grief, near the spot where the mail has been upset more than once. The ascent of the Ord tried the metal of the bicyclists, but they had compensation in the splendid run down the hill to Berriedale. Their halt at Wick lasted three-quarters of an hour, when, after a hasty dinner, they started for John o'Groats, which they reached soon after nine o'clock on Monday, apparently little the worse for their long, interesting, and unexampled bicycle journey. Eight hundred miles in 14 days is a pretty good illustration of the practical value of the Bicycle.

AMATEUR BICYCLING CHAMPIONSHIP.

1871.

The first race for the championship was held at Lillie Bridge, on the 17th August, 1871, under the auspices of the Athletic Club. The distance was four miles, and Mr. H. P. Whiting, though opposed by one or two other competitors, had not the slightest difficulty in winning; the time, 16 minutes, 25 seconds, showing how little he had to fear from them.

1872.

This year Mr. Whiting did not compete for the championship, the contest for which took place in March, with the following result :—J., T. Honeywell, 1, G. C. Kerr 2, J. E. Copeland 3. Time, 17 minutes, 25½ seconds.

1873,

The race for the championship this year was held on the 3rd of April, and brought out no fewer than seven competitors, of whom H. P. Whiting proved *facile princeps*, doing remarkably good time. The following was the result of the race :—

H. P. WHITING, A.A.C.	(51-inch wheel)	1
G. FRITH, Putney	(56 ,, ,,)	2
R. T. CAUSTON, Surrey B.C.	(53 ,, ,,)	3
C. R. CRIPPS, Liverpool	(53 ,, ,,)	0
J. D. CHARRINGTON	(55 ,, ,,)	0
J. REVELL, jun. St. George's B.C.	(42 ,, ,,)	0
G. C. KERR, Richmond	(50 ,, ,,)	0

Time, 14 minutes, 37 seconds.

1874.

Again H. P. Whiting proved victorious in the race run on the 26th of March, though till the last lap he was held by G. Smith, Surrey Bicycle Club. The following five comprised the field :—

H. P. WHITING, A.A.C.	1
G. SMITH, Surrey B.C.	2
J. WARRINGTON, St. George's B.C.	0
A. MEEK, A.B.C.	0
J. COPLAND, Surrey B.C.	0

Time, 14 minutes, 56 seconds.

AMATEUR CHAMPIONS.

			Min.	Secs.
1871	H. P. WHITING	Time	16	25
1872	J. T. HONEYWELL	,,	17	$25\frac{1}{2}$
1873	H. P. WHITING	,,	14	37
1874	H. P. WHITING	,,	14	56

AMATEUR BICYCLING.

In June, 1870, Mr. C. Mansel and Mr. Crofts started from Wimbledon at 6.30 a.m., and rode to Brighton, returning the same day, *via* Croydon, to Wimbledon, which they reached at 10.30 p.m., having covered 103 miles in 14 hours.

In July, a rider undertook the journey from Aberdeen to London, but was obliged to stop on reaching Moulton Eangate, after nine days, having averaged $59\frac{1}{2}$ miles per diem.

On Monday, August 15th, 1870, two riders started to perform the journey to Bath and back from Blackfriars' Road, which they left at 5.55 a.m., reaching Hungerford, where they stopped the night, at 9.40. The rest of the journey was performed as follows :—Tuesday, Hungerford to Bath ; Wednesday, Bath to Marlborough ; Thursday, Marlborough to Wokingham ; Friday, Wokingham to London. They thus covered 216 miles in five days, which was then a fair performance.

In May, 1871, J. Meere, Paris, is said to have ridden from Paris to Rouen, a distance of 90 miles, in ten hours and a half.

Three members of the Amateur Bicycle Club started from Amesbury on the morning of September 2nd, 1871, and visited Stonehenge, from whence they proceeded through Marlborough, and arrived in London the same night, having accomplished a little over 100 miles in the day.

The following expedition was performed by some members of the Amateur Bicycle Club, in the Autumn of 1871.

1st day—Putney to Oxford.
2nd „   Oxford to Gloucester.
3rd „   Gloucester to Chepstow (*via* Ross, Monmouth, and
              the Valley of Wye).
4th „   Chepstow to Abergavenny.
5th „   Abergavenny to Carmarthen (*via* Brecon).
6th „   Carmarthen to Aberayron (*via* Lampeter).
7th „   Aberayron to Aberystwith (*via* Devil's Bridge).
8th „   Aberystwith to Dolgelly.
9th „   Dolgelly to Festiniog (*via* Bala).
10th „   Bala to Bangor (*via* Carnarvon)
11th „   Bangor to Conway.
12th „   Conway to Chester (*via* Abergele and St. Asaph).

The return journey from Chester to London occupied five days, the nights being passed at Llanrwst, Shrewsbury, Worcester, and Oxford. During the tour, no great day's performance was done; yet still a long distance was traversed, and the party had time to visit objects of interest, as well as to enjoy the lovely scenery of the districts through which they went.

In 1872 a member of the A.B.C. went from London to Ascot on the Cup Day, saw most of the races, and rode back to town, having averaged 10 miles an hour.

On July 4th, 1872, "Dauntless" rode from Liverpool to London, 206 miles, in two days, on a 48-in. Spider.

NOTES ON THE ROAD.

Liverpool to Prescot, 8 miles good road. There is a capital road until within 6 miles of Newcastle-under-Lyne, then a very bad bit, full of holes. This road as far as Stone is very open and fatiguing in hot weather. After leaving Lichfield there is a very trying road, short lengths being good and bad alternately. Coleshill to Coventry the road is very good, but between Daventry and Towcester indifferent, with several steep inclines. From Dunstable the road tends to be hilly for some distance, and then undulates as far as St. Alban's.

On the 19th September, 1872, the first race from London to Brighton came off between thirteen members of the A.B C., and was won by Hunt (38-in. wheel) , Temple (44-in.), who was allowing the winner a considerable start, came in second, making the best time of the party, 5 hours, 25 minutes.

About the same time, C. E. J., a member of the A.B.C., tried a bicycle tour in France. Starting from Dieppe, he rode to Serifontaine, thence to St. Denis and Paris. Starting from St. Denis, he went to Meru Songéaus, Abbeville, and home *via* Montreuil to Boulogne. The chief drawback to the success of the tour was the bad condition of the roads in many places, the *pavée* being especially unsuitable for bicycling.

Mr. W. F. J. Potts performed the following journey in September, 1872 :—

1st day	... ...	London to Kettering	... ... 75 miles.
2nd ,,	... ...	Kettering to Doncaster	... ... 174 ,,
3rd ,,	... ...	Doncaster to Thirsk	... ... 245 ,,
4th ,,	... ...	Thirsk to Sunderland	... ... 287 ,,

The distances done each day were—1st day, 75 miles; 2nd day, 100 miles; 3rd day, 70 miles; 4th day, 42 miles; the whole distance from London to Sunderland, 287 miles, taking $3\frac{1}{2}$ days.

In the same month Mr. Charles Wheaton, of the Surrey Bicycle Club, rode from London to Newcastle, 274 miles, in three days, the daily journeys being as follow :—

1st day	... ...	London to Stamford	... ... 89 miles.
2nd ,,	... ...	Stamford to York	... ... 196 ,,
3rd ,,	... ...	York to Newcastle	... ... 264 ,,

1st day, 89 miles; 2nd day, 107 miles; 3rd day, 58 miles. He rode a 46-in. machine.

In the spring of 1873, the journey from Mansfield to London, a distance of 144 miles, was accomplished by a gentleman in $18\frac{1}{2}$ hours. He set out at 1 a.m., and passing Newark, Grantham, Stamford, Stilton, Huntingdon, Royston, Ware, and Tottenham, reached London at 7.30 p.m.

In May, 1873, Mr. Honeywell, the Amateur champion of the previous year, started from Surbiton, on a 46-in. machine, at 4.45 a.m., and passing through Bagshot, Basingstoke, Romsey, and Lychett, reached Wareham at 9.5 p.m., thus covering 110 miles in a little over 16 hours, including stoppages.

In August, 1873, a match between the Surrey and Middlesex Bicycle Clubs, was ridden from London to Brighton and back. Six members of each club contended, a prize being given to the club whose united members did best, and another for the first in the races. The following were the competitors :—

Surrey.

R. T. Causton	(50-inch wheel)
W. Biddlecombe	(53 „ „)
A. Howard	(48 „ „)
C. Wheaton	(48 „ „)
A. Ward	(50 „ „)
H. E. Watson	(48 „ „)

Middlesex.

G. Pearce	(47-inch wheel)
E. Kennedy	(48 „ „)
C. Leaver	(45 „ „)
A. Walker	(50 „ „)
H. Walker	(50 „ „)
W. Wood	(52 „ „)

The first to arrive home was W. Wood, who is said to have made the quickest time on record—134 miles in 11 hours. He was followed by Causton and Ward, thus securing the victory for Surrey, though the Middlesex Club supplied the first man.

In September, 1873, a party of the Surrey Club rode from London to Brighton, on to Worthing and home, stopping one night on the way.

On the 13th September, two members of the Pickwick Bicycle Club accomplished the journey from London to Land's End in 58 hours, including stops.

Starting from London on the 22nd of September, Mr. H. M. Jones and Mr. W. J. F. Potts, both of the Tension Bicycle Club, performed the following nine days' journey, riding 48-in. machines.

1st day	... ...	London to Stamford	... ...	$88\frac{1}{4}$ miles.
2nd „	... ...	Stamford to Went Bridge	...	$171\frac{1}{2}$ „
3rd „	... ...	Went Bridge to Greta Bridge		$241\frac{1}{2}$ „
4th „	... ...	Greta Bridge to Carlisle	...	300 „
5th „	... ...	Carlisle to Lanark	... ...	376 „
6th „	... ...	Lanark to Auchterarden	...	430 „
7th „	... ...	Auchterarden to Burntisland		477 „
8th „	... ...	Burntisland to Jedborough ...		536 „
9th „	... ...	Jedborough to Sunderland ...		606 „

1874.

January.—Messrs. Ward and Watson rode a race from Croydon to Brighton, the former being allowed 5 minutes start. Roads were very heavy, and rain and snow excessive. Ward won by 10 minutes.

February.— Mr. J. Revell, jun., of St. George's Club, rode from Brighton to Kennington, against Mr. Gregory, walking 20 miles, but lost.

April 27th.—The following gentlemen rode from Brighton to London :—

	In.	Time.	Remarks.
A. Howard	50	5 hours 25 min.	
C. Wheaton	47	5 „ 41 „	Wheaton received ¼-hour
W. Biddlecombe ...	53	6 „ 10 „	start.
G. Sewell	50	6 „ 1 „	
A. Ward	50	6 „ 18 „	

April 21st.—"Brefney" rode a 54½-in. from Portsmouth to Brighton, in 4 hours, 7 mins., 30 sec.; distance 48 miles.

April.—Henry Wilson and Wm. McCann rode a race from Sheffield to Plymouth for £50. Wilson won, owing to collapse of McCann's bicycle.

April.—Mr. St T. M., London to Market Rasen on a 50-inch. Time, 23 hours.

NOTES ON THE ROAD.

Alconbury, Weston Hill, descent by Sawtry, was very rough. From Peterboro' to Market Deeping the road was very bad, but gradually improved to Spalding. From Rivesby to Horncastle nearly all loose flint, and this portion of the road requires careful riding; after this the road degenerates into two-wheel ruts and a horse track, driving being sometimes utterly impossible. From Bennieworth to North Willingham the road improves considerably, but the three miles following into Rasen are as bad as bad can be.

April 1874.—A gentleman of the Pickwick Bicycle Club rode 156 miles in less than 23 hours, inclusive of rest and refreshment.

April—Lillie Bridge Ground, St. George's Bicycle Club.

ONE MILE HANDICAP.

Name.	Diameter.	Yds. start.	Result.
A. Gee	50-in.	30	1
J. Warrington	52	scratch	2
F. V. Honeywell	47	20	—
J. Revell, jun.	50	35	—
W. James	48	95	—

Time—3 minutes, 40 seconds.

TEN MILE AMATEUR HANDICAP.

Name.	Diameter.	Yds. start.	Result.
R. T. Causton	54	300	1
H. P. Whiting	51	scratch	2
J. Warrington	45	520	3
A. Meek	50	525	—
T. B. Frith	53	580	—
A. Gee	50	710	—
C. Howard	50	750	—
G. R Oxx	49	800	—
F. Shew	48	820	—

Time—37 minutes, 20 seconds.

May.—I. K. Falconer rode from Bournemouth to Hitchin, on a 53-in.—distance, 135 miles. Time occupied, including stoppages, 19¼ hours; excluding stoppages, the journey was accomplished at the average rate of 8⅞ miles per hour.

May.—H. S. Thorpe rode from Hertford to Coventry and back; distance to Coventry 82 miles. Time, 9 hours, 40 min. The whole distance (there and back), 164 miles, in 22 hours, 55 min. A 50-in. bicycle was used.

NOTES ON THE ROAD.

After 12 miles ride St. Alban's presents a steep hill, with a very sharp turn at the bottom and a rough road. From Dunstable there is a nice run of a mile, leading by an undulating road to Hockliffe, where you meet with another steep hill; continuing the journey over undulating ground to Brickhill, there is a mile-and-a-half descent to Fenny Stratford (35 miles); then for 7 miles the distance between Fenny Stratford and Stony Stratford, the road is hilly and rough. Towcester and Weedon again yield some long hills. From Dunchurch to within 4 miles of Coventry there is a nice level run.

May 22nd.—Mr. Eden, of Oriel, and the "Dark Blue" Bicycle Club, won a 1-mile race, in 3 min. 10 sec.

May 30th—Surrey Bicycle Club met to decide ONE MILE HANDICAP, open to Youths not exceeding 17 years of age.

Name.	Start.	Result.
E. Burgess	70 yards.	1
R. Temple	scratch	2
C. Graham	50 yards	3
D. Huzzard	135 „	—
G. Boden	140 „	—

Time—3 minutes, 46 seconds.

ONE MILE HANDICAP, without using Handles.

H. P. Whiting 1
R. Causton 2
J. Copland 3

Three other gentlemen started.

FOUR MILES HANDICAP.

Name.	Yds. start.	Diameter.	Result.
H. P. Whiting	scratch	50	1
G. Smith	200	55	2
R. Causton	110	56	3

Twelve other gentlemen ran. Time—13 minutes, 45 seconds.

SIX MILES HANDICAP.

Name.	Yds. start.	Diameter.	Result.
R. Causton	125	56	1
H. P. Whiting	scratch	50	2

Six other gentlemen ran. Time—22 minutes, 5¼ seconds,

Two Mile Handicap.

Name.			Yds. start.	Diameter.	Result.
G. Smith	...	...	...	scratch	55	1
H. C. Howard	...	...	...	100	50	2
G. R. Oxx	...	...	...	120	53	3

Time—8 minutes, 5 seconds.

Match between H. P. Whiting, Amateur Champion (scratch), and R. Causton (200 yards). Distance 10 miles. H. P. Whiting won.

Time—5 miles   ...   21 minutes, 50 seconds.
  „   10   „   ...   42   „   9   „

June 1st.—Oxford to Dunstable and back was accomplished in 9 hours, including 1 hour 35 min. for stoppages.   The whole distance is 86 miles.   The time occupied in going there (43 miles) was 3 hours, 50 min.

June.—Brighton to Horley and back—a distance of 63 miles, was enjoyed by 31 riders.   This trip was run on the 60th birthday of Mr. Bucknell, who rode all the distance.   The youngest of the party was only $13\frac{1}{2}$ years of age, and he too rode the whole distance, on a 36-in. diameter bicycle.

June.—Newbury to Brighton and back.—Messrs. Martin, Simmonds, Cave, and Adey, run this trip on the way down, *via* Odiham, Farnham, Guildford, Horsham, and Henfield (a distance of 85 miles) and back, *via* Cuckfield, Crawley, Reigate, Kingston, and Reading, a distance of 106 miles.

June.—Bristol to London.—Mr. Sidney Isaac, of Maldon, Essex, rode a 48-in. bicycle to the Marble Arch.   Stoppages occupied $5\frac{1}{4}$ hours; so the distance (122 miles) was done in 14 hours, 35 min., average rate being $8\frac{1}{3}$ miles per hour.

July 18th.—A member of the Cambridge Club rode from Nottingham to Cambridge, *via* Loughborough, Leicester, Market Harborough, Kettering, and Huntingdon.

NOTES ON THE ROAD.

The worst portion of this road lies between Nottingham and Loughboro'. From Loughboro' to Leicester the surface is loose granite; but thence to Market Harboro' it is capital.   Between Harboro' and Kettering there are a few short but trying hills.   Half way between Thrapstone and Huntingdon at first it is rather loose on the surface, but soon alters into a well-made gravel road.   Huntingdon to Cambridge is considered the finest road in England for bicyclists, being very level and smooth.

July.—" Banshee " run from Shepherd's Bush to Tunbridge Wells, 42 miles in 6 hours.

NOTES ON THE ROAD.

The weather being wet, he found the roads after Herne Hill very pasty, **very** indifferent to Bromley ; and worse to Farnboro', after which there is a long pull of about 4 miles up-hill to " Polhill Arms."

Saturday, July 18th.—A race was arranged to take place between **Mr. A. Meek**, of Wrest Park, Shefford, and the Hon. I. Keith Falconer, of the Vicarage, Hitchin.   The course extended over 10 miles, the starting-point being the first milestone on the Bedford road, and the winning-post the fourth milestone beyond Shefford, on the same road.   Meek appeared on a splendid 52-in. racing bicycle, built by Keen, of Surbiton, weighing but 40-lbs.; whilst Falconer rode his ordinary roadster, 53-in. diameter, built by Thomas Sparrow, of Knights-bridge, weighing over 60-lbs.   Meek's weight is 11-st. 6-lbs., Falconer's 15-st. It will be seen, therefore, that Meek had a decided advantage in point of weight.   It is, however, worthy of notice, that Meek's machine was not his own, but one lent for the occasion ; he, consequently, suffered the disadvantage of riding a machine strange to him. The start was made at eleven minutes past six p.m.   The Hitchin man immediately showed to the front, running away at a tremendous pace, which he kept up for nearly half the distance, covering the first four miles in 15 minutes.   Meek all the time was following at a moderate pace, reserving his strength for the part beyond Shefford, most of which was up-hill.   On arriving at the railway bridge, Meek met with an accident, a stone catching the wheel ; it swerved, and ran against the stone-work of the bridge, precipating the rider, who thus lost a minute or more.   He, however, re-mounted, and continued the race.   He did not succeed in catching up Falconer, who won the race, completing the 10 miles in 38 minutes.   Meek reached the post 5½ min. later.

July.—W. H. Oxley rode from Land's End to within a few miles of Manchester.   Time and distance are not recorded, the trip being simply to see the country.   We are able, however, to add a few valuable

NOTES OF THE ROAD.

Land's End to Penzance, 10 miles of really good road, with only one or two moderate hills ; thence all the way to Plymouth, a distance of 90 miles, the roads are capital, undulating only sufficiently to create a rest.   Plymouth to Exeter, *via* Brent, Ashburton, and Chudleigh, is also a good road for the whole distance, though hilly in portions. Exeter to Bath, 75 miles, the road is at first good ; but at Wells troubles begin ; approaching Bath the hills are steep and long.   Bath to Shrewsbury, the roads are pretty level, most parts being very good.   Shrewsbury to Nantwich is simply execr..ble, and for 45 miles further ; after which, the road to Manchester is good,

July—Surrey Bicycle Club, FOUR MILE RACE, for the Captaincy and Sub-Captaincy.

Name.			Diameter.	Result.	Remarks.
R. T. Causton	...	... ...	51	1	By 6yds. clear.
J. H. Sewell	...	... ...	50	2	
A. Ward	...	... ...	52	—	
H. C. Howard	...	... ...	52	—	

ONE MILE HANDICAP.

Name.			Diameter.	Yds. start.	Result.
H. C. Howard	...	... ...	52	35	1
J. Copland	...	... ..	52	10	2
G. R. Oxx	...	... ...	53	30	3

Three other gentlemen rode. Time—3 minutes, 32 seconds.

FIVE MILES, FOR WHITING CHALLENGE CUP.

Name.			Diameter.	Yds. start.	Result.
H. C. Howard	...	... ...	52	380	1
J. Copland	...	... ...	52	310	2
W. Biddicombe	...	... ...	55	550	3
R. T. Causton	...	... ...	51	scratch	—
A. Ward	...	... ...	52	300	—
T. C. Holloway	...	... ...	50	400	—
G. R. Oxx	...	... ...	53	440	—

Time—19 minutes, 48 seconds.

RACE FROM BATH TO LONDON.

On the first Monday in August, the race for the captaincy and sub-captaincy of the Middlesex Bicycle Club took place, from Bath to London, a distance of 106 miles. The start was from the front of the Abbey, and all the competitors were up to time. Mr. Thomas Sparrow, who accompanied the race, started them at 5.8, and owing to the great number of people assembled, there was some difficulty in passing through the crowds. In a few minutes, however, they were out of the town, and the running was very sharp. Walker and Tyne were leading. Some of the competitors had to dismount and walk up Box Hill. They all passed through Chippenham, at the rate of 14 miles per hour, and Calne (19 miles) was reached in 1½ hour. They passed through in the following order :—Walker, Leaver, Tyne, Percy, Goulding, Spencer, Pearce. No stoppage was made until Marlborough (32 miles), was reached, Walker, Tyne, and Leaver, coming in together, the distance being got over in 2¾ hours. Spencer here passed Sparrow and Goulding. From Marlborough and Newbury (18 miles), Walker and Tyne led the way, Pearce overhauling them in Savernake Forest. Walker and Tyne performed the journey from Bath to Newbury (50 miles) in 4¾ hours. Leaver and Percy were making good time as far as Woolhampton ; but soon afterwards Leaver dropped back, and was passed by

Spencer at Reading. Walker soon after made a spurt, and Tyne saw no more of him. At Twyford Spencer overhauled Percy, whence they had a smart race as far as Colnbrook, where Percy stopped to rest. The arrivals at the club-room at Kensington were—

Walker, 3.15 p.m. | Tyne, 5.50 p.m. | Spencer, 6.12 p.m.
Percy, 6.58 p.m. | Leaver, 7.35 p.m.

On Monday, August 4th, there was a race from the "Albion," Brighton, to the "Swan and Sugarloaf," Croydon, between members of the Surrey B.C. and St. George's B.C. During the race there was a strong wind blowing from the N.W., which considerably reduced the speed, and increased the labour of the riders. Distance 41 miles.

	Order.	Time.	
		hrs.	min.
Holloway	1	3	45
Gee	2	3	53
Revell	3	4	0
Howard	0	4	5
Oxx	0	4	10

August 3rd.—Greenock to Ingleton, Lancashire.—"Tortoise" left Greenock, rode through Largs to Ardrossan ; the roads were level close to the Clyde, up as far as Ardrossan and Kirkconnel. Through Kilwinnin, Irwin, Mauchline and Old and New Cumnock, the roads are hilly and rough, but from Kirkconnel to Dumfries through Sanquhar and Thornhill there is fine scenery and capital roads. From Dumfries to Annan is rather hilly, but the roads are not bad. From Annan to Carlisle, through Gretna, he says, his "bicycle almost ran away with *him*" (Gretna is noted for runaway matches.) Carlisle to Penrith the road is hilly, but good going; Penrith to Pooley Bridge hilly and rough ; Pooley Bridge to Patterdale by the side of Ulleswater, flat. Over Kirkstone Pass to Ambleside it is simply unfit for a bicycle. Thence to Kirby Lonsdale the roads are good, but from there to Ingleton hilly and rough.

RACE FROM KENNINGTON TO WALTON.

In September—Open Handicap for two prizes. Course, from Kennington Oval along the Clapham and Balham roads to the double gates at Merton, through Combe Lane to Norbiton, over Kingston and Hampton Court bridges, through East and West Moulsey, past Apps Court, through Walton-on-Thames to Oatlands Park. Distance, over 17 miles. The roads not in good order—slippery where watered, and dusty where dry. Causton and Nevill started scratch, and, going at a slow pace, kept together till nearing Merton level crossing, where Causton went ahead and gradually caught up all his men, with the exception of Fletcher (S.B.C.) who won easily; Copland (S.B.C.) who was second; and Gee, of the St. George's B.C. who was third. No time taken.

At a meeting of the Surrey B.C., six events were set down for decision. Four miles' open race, T. Sabin† (Coventry), and T. Fletcher,† (S.C.B.) G. R. Oxx won the Mile Handicap. Five Miles' Handicap, to H. C. Howard. One Mile Handicap, open to Boys under 16 years of age, was won by Alfred Keen.

September.—T. H. H. rode a 48-inch machine from Banbury to Whitchurch, Salop. Distance 103 miles

NOTES ON THE ROADS.

Avoid the more direct road from Banbury to Warwick, as it is in wretched condition, but Banbury to Leamington is all that can be desired. The road between Birmingham and Wolverhampton is very bad and wearying ; in fact it is full of holes and tramway ruts. The bicyclist had better train this bit. Wolverhampton to Newport is, on the whole, good ; thence to Thornhill, also good, but from this to Whitchurch Heath it is bad.

September.—B. H. C. rode from Nottingham to Edinburgh, in six days.

NOTES ON THE ROAD.

From Nottingham to Mansfield there are 14 miles of excellent road, but thence to Doncaster, stiff clay, very rutty and uneven. Tadcaster to York, it is quite impassable. The road from York to Knavesborough, is in some places three inches deep in mud, but improves to Ripley, and thence to Ripon is perfect. You can now ride splendidly till within 10 miles of Darlington. The roads from Darlington through Durham, to Newcastle-on-Tyne, though hilly, are both good and firm. Newcastle to Berwick, a distance of 65 miles, covers a most excellent road, and yields some beautiful scenery. Berwick to Edinburgh is also an excellent piece of ground, but between Dunbar and Haddington there is one very long hill.

October.—Jas. T. R. Wood accomplished the task of riding from *London to Bath* AND BACK, in 37 hours with only one hour's sleep ; this with 8½ hours for stoppages, leaves 27½ hours of continuous treading.

October.—L. A. B. C. in 5 days, rode from London to Sunderland, a distance of 401 miles.

NOTES ON THE ROAD.

Newport Pagnall to Northampton, the road is rough, but improves on the way to Lutterworth. Wigan to Newcastle, with the exception of a few miles, is good, but towards Kendal the road is almost impassable. From Carlisle to Sunderland, a distance of 70 miles, it is impassable after dark.

THROUGH WALES AND IRELAND.

On the 26th of August I started from the "Raven" Hotel, Shrewsbury, on a bicycling tour through Wales and round the north of Ireland. My luggage weighed 19-lbs., and my bicycle was a 40-in. wooden-wheeler. I ran over Mont ford Bridge, passed Oswestry on my left, and arrived at the picturesque ruins of the Castle at Whittington. In Chirk I halted at the "Hand" Hotel. The roads were good from Chirk to Llangollen and Corwen. From Corwen the driving is all against the collar to a mile and a half or two miles beyond Curig-y-Druidion. Leaving Curig-y-Druidion, next morning, Pentre-Voelas was shortly reached. I continued my ride to the Conway Falls and the Fairies' Glen as far as Bettws-y-Coed. After a halt of an hour I rode up the pass to the Swallow Falls, and found a continued ascent to Capel Curig, thence to Pent-y-gwryd at the foot of Snowdon and entrance to Llanberris Pass. The road was followed to the top of Llanberris Pass, down the other side of which I rattled along at a lively pace to the "Royal Victoria" Hotel at Llanberris. The journey was continued along the lake side through Cwym-y-Glo and Llanrug to Carnarvon. The road to Capel-Curig is excellent, though rather sharp up-hill from Bettws-y-Coed. From Capel-Curig to Llanberris it becomes almost exactly like a Scotch mountain, or Highland road, but sufficiently good for men who ride well-built machines, and are not great at grumbling. From Llanberris to Carnarvon a more muddy surface had to be run over. From Carnarvon I took the road towards Beddgelert, and arrived there in time for lunch ; and then the nag was trotted down the Aberglaslyn Pass, say about a couple of miles out over Pont Aberglaslyn, on the Festiniog road, then back over the bridge,, and a few hundred yards down the road to Tremadoc, and back to Beddgelert. From the latter place the run was continued up the pass, skirting in succession the two very beautiful little lakes of Dinas and Gwinant, and up the head of the valley to Pent-y-Gwryd. Soon after half-past nine, I took the road for Holyhead *via* Bangor, where I was agreeably surprised to find excellent quarters at the "George." Went on board the "Edith," August 31st, at Holyhead, for Greenore, where I had determined to attack Ireland.

At 9.15 on the morning of Monday, Aug. 31st, I was landed at the dirty and partly-civilised town of Warrenpoint, after passing the beautiful scenery of Rostrevor. About half-past ten o'clock I started for Newry, over a wide road, with a footpath upon which there is good going in places. I found nothing particularly worth stopping for in the dirty moderate-sized town of Newry, out of which runs what the Irish call a "grand" road to Belfast. There can be no doubt that the road is very grand if width has anything to do with it, but the surface is pitiably kept, and there are not above two or three miles of it on the Belfast side of Dromore where anything like high speed can be attained. Banbridge was made half-way house this day, and, passing through Dromore, I pulled up at Hillsborough. Continuing the run to Belfast, the road was found pretty in the neighbourhood of Lisburn ; but the surface is little or no better than the inferior macadamised London roads; and in Belfast itself the jolting is simply distressing.

To avoid a further jolting in Belfast, and having ascertained that the roads, from Larne, along the Antrim coast, were good, I left Belfast by the 6.10 a.m. train on Sept. 1st., for Larne. The road skirts the beautiful sea-coast of County Antrim all the way. The character of the whole line of road is rather rough on the surface, with occasional land springs bursting through; but generally it is well built, and metalled with hard dark-looking freestone. From Cushendall to Cushendun the road makes nearly a semi-circle inland, rising high over the hills from Cushendun Bay in a circuitous manner, for about four miles on to peat and heather land, whence it descends for about four or five Irish miles at a stretch, to Ballycastle. Leaving Ballycastle, the Bushmills road was taken, which proved to be more or less straight, over peat bogs, and uninteresting. At Bushmills, McIlroy's Hotel afforded comfortable and well-provisioned quarters, after a day of nearly sixty miles.

On September 2nd, the Giant's Causeway was reached. I then took the road along the coast to Port Rush. Passing Port Rush, I took the road to Coleraine.

There are two big Irish roads from Coleraine, leading over the hills some hundreds of feet up, and then down again to New Town, Limivady. Of the two roads, the one more inland was taken on the recommendation of local authorities, and found to be in such an execrable state of repair, and so badly engineered, that driving along it in many places was positively dangerous. Beyond Limavady (or New Town, as it is there called) the road to Londonderry is good; footpaths, however, prove welcome enough.

On Sept. 3rd I left Derry, after a good night's rest, for Strabane, and started along the valley of the river Finn to Stranorlar and Ballybofey. Thence I rode over the hills and through the "gap" to Donegal.

Next day I started from Donegal to Ballyshannon; pulled up at Brownhall. Ballyshannon was reached about mid-day. From Ballyshannon to Belleek the going was of a most slippery and slow nature, over a road covered with a thick layer of slime, so that great difficulty was experienced in proceeding at all. From Belleek, which is located quite at the lower end of Lower Lough Erne, the road to Enniskillen was so bad that no two hundred yards at a stretch could be found where any respectable pace could be indulged in; and, moreover, it was dangerous not to try and drive up the short sharp hills, because the dips between them were so slippery, that an almost certain spill would have followed an attempt to dismount.

Leaving Enniskillen on the 7th of September, I passed Loughs Nilly and Macnean, and ran through a place called Manor Hamilton. The first nine miles of this road were Irish (2580 yards each), slimy, and bad for bicycling; then came a change for the better, and the road through Manor Hamilton to Sligo proved very fair, and was marked out in English statute miles.

Next day I found between Sligo and Ballina an uninteresting and bad, although seemingly well-used road. The "Victoria" Hotel at Sligo gave me fair accommodation, but at Ballina I should prefer some other house to the Moy. When I had got over the thirty-seven miles of road in the forenoon, with little to see for my trouble, the rain having set in heavily, I determined to ship myself and steed aboard the train for Westport.

Taking the road to Lenane, I entered the Connemara county, but found the roads rapidly improving, and at Lenane I made some rapid running.

The following day I rode over to Kylemore Castle and back to Lenane (eighteen English miles over the hills) to breakfast at 9.40. I started then for a ride over the hills to Cong, at the head of Lough Corrib. The road from Lenane to Kylemore was capital, as, indeed, it continued to within three miles of Cong. The running this day was easy, mostly down hill and with the wind aft, so that all the local runners from the roadside hovels or cabins were utterly outpaced, even up the hills. Most of the roads among the Galway Hills are really excellent, and quite equal to those in Scotland. It is wrong to call the roads of County Antrim superior. The roads to Cong were of the limestone class, so I decided to take the steamer to Lough Corrib, to convey me and my bicycle to Galway. Thence I came on to Dublin by train, landed at Holyhead on the 15th, and went to Bangor.

Starting at the British Hotel, Bangor, on September 15th, I took the Conway road, which proved very deficient in top dressing, and was distressingly bumpy, to within a few miles of Conway, where it improved. The "Castle" Hotel at Conway is a comfortable house. From Conway to Llanwrst the road on the west side of the river is not good.

Next morning I started from Lanwrst, at 10.30, and rode over a capital road on the eastern bank of the Conway to Waterloo Bridge, just beyond Bettws-y-Coed; whence the run was continued over a very fair road for mountain work. The descent into Festiniog,—through a mass of formidable-looking slate quarries, intersected by a very narrow gauge line of railway, threading itself in and out of the hills in quite a comically serpentine manner,—is too steep to ride down all the way with safety, From Festiniog to Dolgelly, a more savage and villainous state of roadway for some twelve miles or so can hardly be looked for in a civilized country. The way to be traversed is in many places no better than a neglected watercourse. The "Golden Lion" and the "Ship" are the two hotels. A start was made on September 17th, and there ensued a charming drive up the valley of the "Union" over a very tolerable road, which was quite a treat after the abominable state of affairs on the previous day. Resuming my seat in the saddle, after a smart, mostly downhill, run of nine miles, I arrived at the Plas Coch, or "Red House" Hotel at Bala.

September 18th, I left this hotel for a climb over the Berwyn Hills, through Llangwenog to Llanrhaidr, the road being generally a mere mountain track. From Llangwenog, I took the longer of the two roads,—which, as often happens, is the better,—to Llanrhaidr. Through Llanrhaidr, I continued my run through Llangedwin, and over another range of hills, much smaller than the Berwyns, to Llansaintfraid, when, after crossing the darkest of brown-looking rivers, Vyrnyw, I found a most exeellent and good-going road to Welshpool, through places called the Four Crosses and Arddleen; so good indeed was this part of the way, that I found no difficulty in riding over the last twelve miles in about sixty-four minutes.

Sept. 19th I started for Bishop's Castle, viâ Chirbury and Church Stoke. The roads were pretty, but rain would have covered the hard, lumpy, limestone roads with a most objectionable and somewhat dangerous slime. From Bishop's Castle, the roads began to improve towards Craven Arms, where they ceased making for the summit of every available hill they could be taken over without diverging a long way from the straight, as had been the case in many places westward of Craven Arms. Through Onibury and Bromfield, a distance of some eight miles into Ludlow, the running had sufficiently improved to be classed as fairly good. The Clee Hill, is very steep, but in tackling it I found a really good freestone road. Having fairly overcome the "the perils of the Clee Hill," ridden down Hopton Bank, as a part of it is called, and passed the last two miles of road in the fag end of the twilight, I landed myself at Cleobury Mortimer. To Tenbury, the roads were unusually heavy. The running improved through Leominster, and to within about six and a half miles of Hereford, where in the parish of Morton, they became extremely distressing, although it crossed a level country. In Hereford there is a most marked contrast, the streets being as near as possible the perfection of smoothness. For the last eight miles between Hereford and Ross the road is decidedly better. The next morning proved fine and sunny, and the road was taken for Monmouth and Tintern. From Tintern I ran on to Chepstow, and thence to Gloucester. From Ross to Monmouth the going is fair, but from Monmouth to Tintern the road is nothing to boast of. From Chepstow the first three miles of the road to Gloucester are beautifully even, as are also the last five or six miles at the Gloucester end. I left Gloucester for Cirencester, and rode along what is called the "Ermine Way" (possibly from its whiteness). This road, grand as it is, was cut too straight by the Romans to allow of its avoiding the many pieces of rising ground that it is taken over; but the condition of the road itself is fairly good. About six miles from Gloucester Birdslip Hill is topped. This is a regular poser—a mile in length—and remarkable for its steepness. Fairford and Lechlade were my two next places of call on the excellent road that runs through both to Wantage. Here I made a halt. Next morning I reached Streatley by ten o'clock. The road leading over the downs out of Wantage to about abreast of Didcot is a credit to those whose duty it is to look after it; but the nine miles west of Streatly do not afford such pleasant going. From

Streatly to Reading there is a capital run, slightly undulating near Basildon. I then chose the road home through Wokingham, Virginia Water, Egham, and Kingston. Leaving Reading I made short work of it over the excellent road through Staines to Kingston. From Kingston to Wimbledon Common, home to South Kensington, there were no special features for remark.

The distances run were, as near as I can measure them, as under: Shropshire and North Wales, 409 miles ; Ireland, 425 miles ; England (on return journey), 174 miles—total, 1,008 miles. And last, but not least, the result of the trip seems to have so thoroughly set me up in health that my friends declare I am in fine training, whilst my expenses were only a few shillings over £25.

These records of Bicycling would be singularly incomplete without a notice of the extremely effective and novel use made of the bicycle in the recent visit of their Royal Highnesses the Prince and Princess of Wales, to Coventry, on the 7th November.—We extract the following from the *Daily Telegraph* of the 9th November. "The bicycle riders were to the fore—for Coventry is, so to speak, the head-quarters of bicyclists. Eighteen of these redoubtable horsemen indeed went forth, not armed *cap a pié* as Coventry men rode out in the olden time, but lightly clad, as cricketers, anxious to give the Royal visitors a welcome such as Coventry men only know how to render. When the Prince and Princess of Wales, at Packington Hall, received a message from the silk-making town, it was on bicycles that the trusty envoys were dispatched. The great packet, with the Corporation seal, went under no convoy of artillery or lancers, was carried in no state or gilded coach, but was trundled pleasantly along in charge of an accomplished bicyclist, who, disdaining the hills and dales which lie between Coventry and Packington, delivered his message with the least possible delay, and swiftly departed." Mr. Thomas, the President of the Coventry Bicycle Association, who had the distinguished honour of acting as Captain on this auspicious occasion, writes to *Land and Water* as follows :—

"I thought it might be interesting to the readers of your paper, who are bicycle riders, to know that the light-winged steeds of steel played their part in the hearty welcome given to the Royal pair—eighteen men of our Club started from head-quarters (both men and machines gaily decorated with the Danish colours,) to ride as far as Meriden Hill, five miles from the town, in order to be the first to welcome our Royal visitors, and also to escort them on their road to Coventry. When the hill was reached a double line was formed, and as the advanced guard of the Royal party appeared, each man sprang to "attention" beside his machine, gave a right hearty cheer while the Royal couple passed, and immediately it had done so, all the men sprang quickly and well on their machines, and followed in two's. The Prince was observed to lean out of his carriage many times and look back at the novel escort, and both their Royal Highnesses seemed pleased and interested, especially when after travelling

about two miles in the manner above-described, all the riders taking advantage
of a foot path, passed the Prince's carriage, and saluting the Royal party as
they passed, which was most graciously acknowledged, four of the party, Messrs.
Thomas, Hickling, Sabin and Townsend, pushed on in front at a great pace, and
announced the approach of the Royal carriage to the Civic authorities within
the pavilion.

Fifteen of the machines were manufactured by the Coventry Machinist Co.,
and four were Ariels."

PROFESSIONAL BICYCLING.

1871.

February 11th, 1871, J. T. Johnson appeared at the Star Grounds, to ride
50 miles, which he had backed himself to do in 4 hours.   As the backer of time
did not put in an appearance, the match did not take place.   Instead, Johnson
rode one mile against time, taking 4 minutes, 2 seconds ; after which, J. Keen
of Surbiton, covered the same distance in 3 minutes, 52·5 seconds.

6th March, at the Star Grounds, Fulham, D. Stanton and W. Howard rode
a 10-mile match.   The former, who received 2 minutes start, won easily, in
47 minutes, 31 seconds.   Both rode 40-inch wheel machines.

May 8th, at Aston Cross Grounds, Birmingham, J. H. Palmer and J. T.
Johnson rode a mile, with 36-inch wheels, for £30.   Palmer won by 10 yards,
in 4 minutes, 2 seconds.

May 20th, at Aston Cross, Mr. T. Cooper's pony, 12h. 1 high, trotted 20
miles, against Johnson (60 inch), and Palmer (52).   At the 98th lap, Palmer
retired, and at the 100th, the pony passed Johnson, who had led till then, and
finally beat him by 30 yards ; time 1 hour, 31 minutes, 10 seconds.

May 29th, at Aston Cross, the race for the one mile championship, after
several heats, was decided as follows :—Johnson, 1 ; Palmer, 2 ; Moore, 3.

August 19th, a match took place between J. Moore, of Paris, riding 400
yards on a bicycle, and J. Nuttall, the champion 600 yards runner, the latter
having to run 390.   After an exciting race, Moore came up at the finish and
won by a short yard, in 45¼ seconds.

September 2nd, a two-mile handicap, in which a number of riders competed,
was won by Johnson, from scratch, his time being 7 minutes, 41½ seconds.

1872.

February 10th, at Aston Cross Grounds, Birmingham. a match took place
between J. Moore, of Paris, and Palmer, of Aston.   The distance was one mile,
and Moore won easily by 50 yards.   Both rode 42-inch machines.

February 22nd, a match for one mile was run between J. T. Johnson and J. H. Palmer, at Aston Grounds; the former on a 36-inch, and the latter on a 40-inch machine. Johnson won by 10 yards, in 3 minutes, 56 seconds.

April 1st, an "All-Comers" handicap, at Aston Grounds, of one mile, was won from scratch by Johnson, in 3 minutes, 26½ seconds.

April 27th, at Queen's Grounds, Sheffield, a match of one mile, between W. Cooper and J. P. Beardsley, was won by the former in 3 minutes, 31 seconds.

May 20th-21st, at the Molineux Grounds, Wolverhampton, the race for the one mile champion cup, resulted as follows :—Shelton, 1 ; Keen, 2 ; Johnson, 3. Won by 10 yards. Time, 3 minutes, 13 seconds.

At the same time a mile handicap was won by Moore, 30 yards start, in 3 minutes, 30 seconds ; Swann (75) being second.

May 18th, at Powderhall Grounds, Edinburgh, A. Bathgate rode a match against J. Miller, for the championship of Scotland. The distance was 5 miles ; and after a most exciting race, Miller won by 5 yards, Time, 23 min, 3 secs.

May 20th, a one-mile handicap for a champion cup, was held at the Melbourne Grounds, Northampton, resulting as follows :—J. Cooper (70 yards start) 1 ; T. Whitehouse (100 yards), 2. Won by 5 yards.

June 17th, at Lillie Bridge, West Brompton, a race for a one-mile challenge cap, was won easily by J. Keen, his opponents being—Markham (2), Lilley, and Hughes. Time, 3 minutes, 57 seconds.

August 3rd, a one mile champion race, took place at the Molineux Grounds, Wolverhampton, resulting as follows :—Keen, 1 ; Shelton, 2 ; Johnson, 0 ; Moore, 0 ; Cooper, 0. Time, 3 minutes, 9½ seconds.

At the same time and place, a mile handicap was won by Moore (20 yards start), Rolfe (120) being second, and Keen (scratch) third.

September 28th, at the same grounds, Keen again won the mile champion cup, with Moore second, Johnson and Shelton being beaten. Time, 3 min. 6¾ sec.

An "all-comers" handicap was also won by Keen from scratch, beating G. Owen (90), and Bank (170).

December 6th, at the same grounds, Keen covered 10 miles in 35 min. 30 sec.

1873.

January 13th, at Lillie Bridge Grounds, an important match was decided between Moore, of Paris, and Johnson, of London. The distance was 50 miles, in which Johnson received 2 miles start. The latter rode a 52-inch machine, while his opponent rode a 49½-inch. After covering 27 miles in 2 hours, 13 minutes, 40 seconds, Johnson retired, leaving Moore to complete the distance in 3 hours, 56 minutes, 40 seconds.

March 1st, a three-mile race, at Aston Cross Grounds, between J. Barlow and H. Hawkesford, was won by the former by 2 yards, in 14 min. 48 sec.

April 14-15, at Molineux Grounds, Wolverhampton, after three trial heats, the mile champion cup was won by Keen, in 3 minutes, 10 seconds, Moore being second, and Shelton third.

In the mile handicap fifty-two competed, the winner turning up in R. Roberts (320 yards' start), with Swann (80) second, Willis. (320) third, and Moore (10) fourth.

April 30th, at the Star Grounds, Fulham, Mr. G. Dixon rode 10 miles against G. Martin, who received ten minutes' start.   The bicyclist won easily.

May 12, at the same grounds, a mile handicap resulted as follows :—C. Lewis (300 yards start), 1 ; S. Perks (220), 2 ; C. Swann (80), 3.

June 3, Keen again met Mr. Cooper's pony, this time on equal terms, over 20 miles.   After going 16 the pony stopped beaten, Keen winning in 1 hour, 17 minutes, 16¼ seconds.

June 1, 2, 3, at the Molineux Grounds, Wolverhampton, the mile championship race resulted as follows :—Keen, 1 ; Cooper, 2.   Time, 3 minutes, 16½ seconds. Moore, Palmer, Johnson, and Shelton also competed.

The mile handicap was won by Whitehouse (220 yards start).

July 7th, at Aston, a race, 20 miles, between Moore and Mr. Cooper's pony, was won by the latter by 140 yards, in 1 hour, 21 minutes.

August 2nd. at the Molineux Grounds, a series of matches were arranged between Keen and Shelton.   1st Match—1 mile, Shelton (25 yards' start) rode over, as Keen fell at the beginning and did not persevere.   2nd match—4 miles. Shelton (200 yards' start), 1.   Won by 80 yards. Time, 13 minutes, 34¾ seconds.

August 16th, at the Molineux Grounds, a match for £50, between Moore and Keen, was decided, Moore to receive 25 yards in a mile.   The latter won by 26 yards, in 3 minutes, 7½ seconds.

At the same time, a mile handicap came off as follows :—Cooper (25 yards start), 1 ; Shelton (20), 2 ; Keen (scratch), 3; Moore (25), 4.   Time, 3 minutes, 9 seconds.

September 27th, 29th, the mile championship race, at the Molineux Grounds, was won by Cooper; Keen, 2; Moore, 3; Shelton, 4.   Time, 3 min. 10¼ sec.

Moore (20 yards' start) won the handicap mile, with the fine time of 2 minutes, 56½ seconds.

October 18th, 20th, there were thirty-seven entries for a mile handicap, at Aston Cross Grounds, the result being :—Hawkesford (180 yards' start), 1 ; Dalton (140), 2 ; Hudson (160), 3 ; Swann (85), 4.   Time, 3 min. 23½ sec.

This was followed by a 4-mile handicap, in which Keen (scratch) was 1 ; Dalton (400), 2; Barlow (400), 3.   Keen won by 50 yards, in 14 min. 50 sec.

A slow race was won also by Keen, and a novice's race by R. Hudson.

1874.

February 2nd, at the Molineux Grounds, a match for £100 was decided between F. Cooper and J. Moore; distance 1 mile; a very close race, was won by Cooper, by 2 yards.   Time, 3 minutes, 9⅖ seconds.

April 6th, at the same grounds, the race for the championship cup was as follows :—J. Moore, 1 ; Keen, 2 ; Shelton, 3.   Won by six inches, in 3 minutes, 2½ seconds.

There were 21 competitors in the mile handicap, which fell to C. T. Williams (220 yards).

April 25th, Bramall Lane, Sheffield, Cooper beat Keen by a yard in a one-mile race for £100.   Time, 3 minutes, 12 seconds.

Moore also beat Shelton over the same distance.

May 2nd, Keen and Cooper again met, at Lillie Bridge, Cooper winning as before.   Time, 3 minutes, 17½ seconds,

May 4th, at the Molyneux Grounds, Keene and Moore rode a mile for £50, Moore winning by 1½ yards, in 3 minutes, 2½ seconds.

The same day, T. T. Williams beat C. Redmond by 20 yards, in 3 minutes, 14¼ seconds.

May 9th, a handicap was run at the Alexandra Grounds, Oldbury, as follows, C. Redmond (150 yards' start), 1 ; J. Hudson (200), 2 ; G. Smith (225), 3.

August 10th, at Molineux Grounds, a mile handicap resulted as follows :— C. Jameson (100 yards) 1 ; J. Keen (scratch), 2 ; W. Cann (120), 3 ; Moore, who came in second, was disqualified for going inside Keen. Time, 2 minutes, 59⅗ seconds.

November 23rd, a 10-mile race, at Lillie Bridge Grounds, between Keen and Stanton, for a Challenge Medal given by the Amateur Bicycle Club. Keen won by 15½ seconds.

November 30th, a 50-mile race, at the Molineux Grounds, Wolverhampton, between Keen and Stanton, for £50 and the Championship, was won by Keen. Time, 3 hours, 9 minutes, and 19 seconds (the fastest on record). Stanton sustained a bad fall at the 31st mile, and retired.

THE MOST REMARKABLE RIDER the Bicycling world has yet produced is, undoubtedly,

DAVID STANTON.

His feat at Lillie Bridge, on 19th October, was, says the *Standard*, the "most extraordinary performance on record of any man, animal, or machine— 106 miles in 7 hours, 58 min., 54½ seconds." We therefore give a complete list of his achievements, as likely to prove both interesting and instructive.

1871.
March 6th.—Beat Howard, 10 miles ; Stanton received 10 minutes start ; Star Grounds, Fulham ; won easily. Time—47 min. 3 sec.
1873.
October 4th.—Beat Stasson, 10 miles ; Tufnell Park, Holloway ; won by 1 yard, Time—37 min. 12 sec.
1874.
July 9th.—Beat Mr. Butcher's "Flying Mary," 5 miles, at Tottenham ; won easily, 19 min. 23 sec.

August 3rd.—Beat Stasson, 10 miles, Tuffnell Park. Time—34 min. 23 sec Won easily.

August 3rd.—Won 2 miles open race without hands, Tufnell Park.

August 10th.—Beat Mr. McDonnell's "Lady Flora," 10 miles, at Enfield ; won easily. Time—36 min. 43½ secs.

Monday, Aug. 17th.—From Bath to London. Time—8 hours, 28 min.

Saturday, Oct. 10th.—Beat Markham, 50 miles, Cremorne Gardens ; won easily.—Time, for 45 miles, 800 yards, 3 hours, 11 min. ½ sec. Markham received 15 minutes start.

Monday, Oct. 19th.—Beat Keen, 106 miles, Lillie Bridge. Time—7 hours, 58 min. 54½ secs. Won easily ; Stanton received 30 min. start.

Oct. 29th.—Won, 10 miles Championship Challenge Cup and Presentation Cup. Won easily. Time—39 min. 5 sec. "Queen of England" Grounds, Hammersmith. His opponents were Markham and Stasson. Keen, who had entered for the race, declined to run.

CHAPTER IV.

Notes on Training.

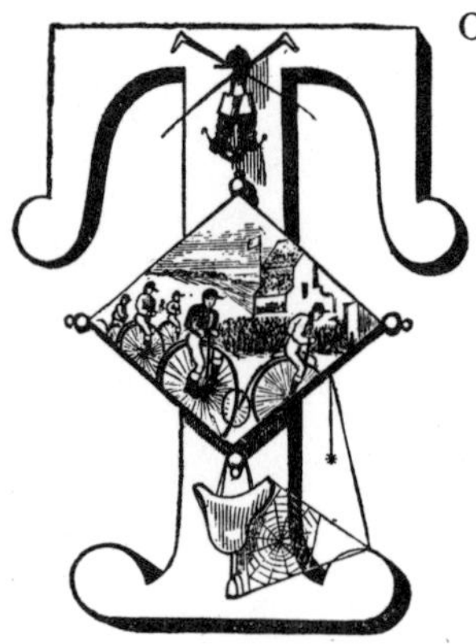

O ATTEMPT any great feat of strength, involving much physical endurance, without previous training, is to court certain failure. Again, no sudden transition from sedentary occupation to a life of vigorous exertion is desirable or safe. The daily amount of exercise should be gradually increased for three or four weeks before strict training commences. The period of preparation for an athletic contest cannot be *too long*, but no great feat of strength should be attempted without a probation of, at the shortest, six weeks duration. It is of course supposed that no one in an abnormal or diseased condition would attempt so severe a trial as is involved in a course of athletic training.

No one who proposes to engage in athletic contests should require physic, either immediately before or during training, for these contests are searching ordeals which none but the healthy can safely undergo. After the first day or two of regular exercise, the stomach and other *viscera*, if free from disease, will perform their various duties without the stimulus of medicine. The day that systematic training commences, the athlete should leave his bed about seven o'clock, and immediately take a cold bath;* not later than eight in the morning, and *before any work has been done*, his breakfast should be served. This meal may consist of broiled or cold roast beef or mutton, chicken, or game. The meat should always be well cooked, and neither under-done nor over-done. There is no better beverage than tea, not taken too hot or strong : green tea should not be used. Those who are not of a bilious habit may substitute milk. No greater quantity of these drinks should be taken than a pint and a half per diem, but this may be supplemented by as much water as is desired. Bread made from flour, which contains the dressing or internal covering of the grain, is better than either bran or fine white bread. Hart's whole-meal bread is the very best.

Active exercise may be commenced about two hours after breakfast, when a good spin on the bicycle, a run, or other strong effort will be well borne. Exercise should be continued, with only short intermissions, until one o'clock; half-an-hour

* The bath is recommended with this limitation : that in summer and winter the temperature shall be preserved the same, and that, under no circumstances, shall the water in winter be used colder than in summer.

will then be occupied in rubbing the skin with hard towels, putting on dry flannels and othewise preparing for dinner.   As a rule, this meal should consist of either broiled or roast meats, but boiled viands may be substituted for them by way of a change.   Game, including venison, pigeons, and wild rabbits, yields much muscle-forming food ; as do beef, mutton, and fowls.   The white-fleshed fishes and trout will serve as an occasional variety, but it is better to avoid the red-fleshed fishes and eels.   Pork, veal, goose, lamb, duck, and all salt meats must not be eaten. A little vegetable may be taken : cauliflower, spinach, peas, and beans are among the most nutritious.   Less vegetable food is required if a little ripe fruit be taken after dinner.   The best drink at this meal is either water or milk.   Small eaters might be allowed a light wine—such as hock or claret—instead of beer ; and now and then most valuable assistance may be obtained for the improvement of the system by a certain quantity of alcoholic stimulant, such as port wine, or half-a-pint of *dry* champagne.   Under all circumstances, if wine is taken at all, it is better that it should be taken at meal times.   In cold weather the food and fluids may generally be more stimulating than in summer.   It is best to exclude all condiments from the training dietary, except salt.   For two or three hours after dinner no severe exertion is permitted, but a quiet stroll, a game of quoits or bowls will be beneficial.

It is a customary practice to get through the most of the daily work of train-ing *before* the principal meal has been eaten.   This is a mistake.   We are in the most favorable condition for great and prolonged muscular exertion *after* this meal has been assimilated ; the reinforced blood is then prepared to replace at once the waste of tissue which all effort, whether mental or muscular, invariably entails.   Nor is the stomach prepared to digest a heavy meal soon after exhaustive exercise, for then the current of blood is diverted to the extremities, and *away* from the stomach, which requires a vigorous circulation in its parietes while performing the important functions of digestion.

THE SEVEREST WORK SHOULD BE UNDERTAKEN DURING THE HOURS INTERVENING BETWEEN DINNER AND SUPPER.

At seven, or half-past past seven, a chop, some cold meat, or oatmeal porridge made with milk, bread, or toast and tea.

The athlete will do well to wean himself from the use of tobacco and fermented liquors, as both should be prohibited when regular training commences. He should also accustom himself to early hours.

Artificial methods of inducing profuse secretions from the skin, by means of packing in wet sheets, extra clothing, &c., are highly objectionable.   Rapid and vigorous exercise is the only healthy method of reducing fat, and in *this* way strength is gained—not lost in the process.

The sleep which we obtain in the early morning hours, as Professor Playfair has shown, is not so valuable as that which we get before twelve at night.   Most men, when working hard, require eight hours' sleep. For these and other reasons, men in training should be in bed by half-past ten o'clock.

It is important to distinguish between sleep and rest, for it is one thing to lie in bed for seven hours and sleep calmly and uninterruptedly, and another thing if slumber is disturbed and a certain amount of rest is substituted for sleep.

It should be a rule that no attempt should ever be made to wake a man in training at any- fixed hour. The duration of sleep must be left entirely to the demands of the system, and should not be interrupted, however long it may continue.

The best general plan to pursue is to discourage any indulgence in rest in bed unless in sleep. As soon as you wake, get up, whether you have had seven hours sleep or not. It will be better, if fatigue is felt, to rest during the day, rather than during the proper hours of sleep.

Leave your bed-room window open at the top at all seasons of the year.

When that condition known as *over-training* comes on, *rest* and port wine should do wonders; if, however, these produce no abatement of the symptoms, consult a physician, and bear this in mind, as our parting injunction : there is no disgrace in yielding to physical weakness; on the contrary, there is more moral courage and true manliness required to wean yourself from a course it might be suicide to pursue, than to follow it blindly and regardless of consequences, rather than bear the taunts of your friends.

DRESS FOR BICYCLING.

For racing, the best dress is that usually worn by runners, consisting of a thin jersey, with knickerbockers, or trousers cut to the knee, made of silk, or some such light material.

The tourist has to take into consideration what is most useful and comfortable for a long ride, as well as what is least likely to hamper his movements. For a long journey, riders will find knickerbockers more comfortable than trousers and gaiters. A flannel shirt and a short yachting coat will complete the costume, [serge is the best wearing material], though a mackintosh strapped to the machine is indispensable. A light gun, or fishing-rod can be tied along the spring, as well as a bag containing sponge, brushes, &c. Thus equipped, a rider may travel for days among the Highlands of Scotland, or through the wildest parts of Ireland.

CHAPTER V.

Golden Rules for Bicycle Riders

NEVER buy a bicycle unless it is of the best quality, and by one of the best makers.

NEVER attempt to ride a bicycle with a driving wheel too large for you.

NEVER fail to thoroughly clean and oil your machine before starting on a journey, and daily when in use.

NEVER use any oil but the best sperm.

NEVER tamper with the adjustment of the wheels, nor take the machine to pieces unnecessarily.

NEVER stir out on your machine without taking with you a spanner and oil-tin.

NEVER turn the wheel of the bicycle from you when the machine has a tendency to fall, but always in the direction in which it is falling.

NEVER travel a long journey without having your drawers lined smoothly and carefully with chamois leather or buckskin.

NEVER fail to get a few hours sleep before starting on a long journey.

NEVER ride in the early morning fasting; a little rum and milk, with an egg beaten up in it, is an excellent sustenant.

NEVER fail if you are in a strange country to ascertain the character of the roads, from natives of the district, before starting.

NEVER ride during the great heat of the sun; but use the early mornings and long summer evenings.

NEVER ride until you are faint, but rest yourself thoroughly at the first indications of exhaustion.

NEVER try how far you can ride without dismounting; a short walk, by bringing a different set of muscles into play, will rest you considerably.

NEVER attempt to ride up the worst hills; you may be able to do so, but it will be better, both for yourself and machine, not to attempt it, especially on a journey.

NEVER place your feet on the rest for a ride down a hill, which you cannot *see all the way to the bottom,* without having your machine thoroughly in hand, in case an immediate dismount become necessary.

NEVER fail to give a wide berth to patchy places in a road.

NEVER fail to lean well forward up hill, and against the wind.

NEVER fail to lean well back on your Bicycle in going down hill.

NEVER ride in the dark, except compelled to do so; unless you know every inch of your road thoroughly.

KNICKERBOCKERS are the best nether garments to ride in, and moderately thick boots are better than thin ones.

NEVER fail, when resting on a journey, to place your machine beyond the reach of meddlesome hands.

CHAPTER VI.

ENGLAND AND WALES.

In compiling the accompanying list of routes, we have most carefully availed ourselves of every scrap of information we could gather from the records of bicycle trips in the newspapers, and from bicyclists themselves; but in the infancy of the movement, the information derivable from these sources is exceedingly limited. We have had, therefore, to rely upon a not inconsiderable personal experience of a great many of the routes, and for the rest we have most carefully studied the various topographical authorities; and we trust the information we have thus been able to impart may prove valuable and beneficial. We have ourselves tested the Hotels to the names of which an asterisk is affixed. ** Denote objects worthy of special attention.

It may be well to mention that all turnpikes are free, except where there is a a toll for pedestrians; in which case the bicyclist has only to pay as a foot passenger.

(Distances are measured from Holborn Viaduct, save where otherwise mentioned.)

Notes on Northern Roads.

From Highgate Archway, to East End, Finchley, is as bad as any rider may wish for, but thence to Barnet, it gradually improves, and at Whetstone the village road is good except for one loose piece. From here to Hatfield the road continues good, though on the other side of the river, there is a gradual ascent of about 2 miles in length. It keeps good down the hill to Welwyn, and quite safe to run down, and useful to do so, as there is an incline at the bottom. The next short bit is rather steep, and caution is necessary in taking the twists of the road. From Welwyn to Hitchin it is undulating, but all the hills can be taken. Hitchin to Biggleswade is a level run of 11 miles. Biggleswade, through Sandy to Tempsford, is very level, and very dreary; here be careful to take the road through St. Neot's, as that through Eaton Socon is loose and bad. St. Neot's to Buckden, the road is fair; Buckden to Huntingdon rather loose. Huntingdon to Alconbury Weston, good but rather hilly, thence to Norman Cross the road is decidedly bad and shakes one excessively. From this to Peterboro' (5 miles) it is much better, but northward, through Deeping Bourne and Sleaford to Lincoln, the roads are very bad, rutty and rough. If possible, avoid all the south western parts of Lincolnshire.

Route I.

LONDON TO PETERBOROUGH.

HIGHGATE ARCHWAY, about 4 miles from LONDON; Whetstone, 6; Green Hill Cross, 10; BARNET, 11; Little Heath Lane, 15; HATFIELD, 19½; Stanborough, 21¼; Welwyn, 25; HITCHIN, 34; BIGGLESWADE, 45; Eaton Socon, 55; Alconbury Hill, 67¾; Stilton, 75; Norman's Cross, 75¾; PETERBOROUGH, 81½.

NOTES ON THE ROAD.

From Highgate under the Archway to East-end Finchley, the road is not a favourite with bicycle riders, but once past there, only one loose piece occurs until Whetstone is reached. A gradient of two miles, gentle in ascent, leads to Barnet, whence Welwyn is reached after rather a steep descent. "Undulating, but good," is the characteristic of the road to Hitchin and Eaton Socon. Thence to Peterborough, somewhat monotonous, but in fair condition.

OBJECTS OF INTEREST

are not numerous on this road, and the bicyclist will find little to detain him. We close the route at Peterborough, because it is a good central *point d' appui* for more extended routes. We do not advise the S.W. Lincolnshire route, which would be the natural continuation of Route I. The scenery is fair, but the roads are very bad.

BARNET.—Obelisk, erected 1740, to commemorate the decisive battle of Barnet, between the Yorkists and Lancasterians, in which the latter were completely defeated, and their leader (Warwick) killed.

HATFIELD.—*Hatfield House, the handsome seat of the Marquis of Salisbury. Queen Elizabeth here received the deputation announcing her accession to the English throne, 1558.

PETERBOROUGH.—**The Cathedral, in which are monuments to the memory of Catharine of Arragon and Mary Queen of Scots, both of whom are buried there. *The house in which Dr. Paley was born.

HOTELS.

Barnet—*Green Man, Red Lion.* Hatfield—*Salisbury Arms, Red Lion.* Hitchin—*Sun.* · Biggleswade—*Swan, Crown.* Peterborough—*Great Northern, Crown.*

Route II.

LONDON TO COVENTRY.

LONDON to BARNET (see Route I), 11 miles; South Mims, 14¾; Ridge Hill, 16; ST. ALBANS, 21; Redburn, 25¼; DUNSTABLE, 33½; BRICKHILL, 43¼; Fenny Stratford, 45; STONEY STRATFORD, 52¼; Old Stratford, 53; TOWCESTER, 60; DAVENTRY, 72¼; Braunston, 75; Dunchurch, 80; Ryton, 86¾; Whitley Bridge, 89½; COVENTRY, 91¼.

NOTES ON THE ROAD.

This road, especially the northern part of it, has undergone many improvements since it was a great coaching highway, and there are only an average number of gradients.

OBJECTS OF INTEREST.

Although passing through a pleasant, diversified country, this road does not afford any very striking scenery. The tourist will probably be detained at St. Albans for the sake of an inspection of the grand old Abbey; in St. Michael's Church there is a monument to the memory of Francis Bacon; and when he arrives at Coventry, there is the all-pervading memory of Leofric's Countess to be duly honoured, Peeping Tom to be contemned, the "three tall spires" to be admired, especially St. Michael's; and the bicycle manufactory of the Coventry Machinists' Company, at Cheylesmore (near the Coventry Railway Station), where the Bicyclist may always be assured of the courteous attention of the manager, Mr. Turner. The Coventry Bicycle Association.

HOTELS.

St. Alban's—*Peahen, George and Dragon.* Dunstable—*Red Lion, *Sugar Loaf.* Fenny Stratford—*Swan, Bull.* Stony Stratford—*Bull, Cock.* Towcester, —*Pomfret Arms, Talbot.* Daventry—*Peacock.* Dunchurch—*Dun Cow.* Coventry—**Castle, King's Head.*

Route III.

LONDON TO HOLYHEAD.

LONDON to COVENTRY, 91¼ miles (see Route II), Stone Bridge, 92¾; BIRMINGHAM, 109½; Soho, 111; Wednesbury, 117½; Bilston, 120; WOLVERHAMPTON, 122¾; SHIFFNAL, 135¼; Watling Street, 141¾; Tern Bridge, 148½; Atcham Bridge, 149¼; SHREWSBURY, 153¼; Nesscliff, 161¾; OSWESTRY, 171¼; Chirk, 177; LLANGOLLEN, 183¾; CORWEN, 194; Cerrig-y-Druidion, 204; Bettws-y-Coed, 216; Capel Cerrig, 221½; BANGOR, 236½; Menai Bridge, 239; Llangristiolus, 246¾; Caer Caeliog, 255¾; Stanley Sands Embankment, 258¼; HOLYHEAD, 260½.

NOTES ON THE ROAD.

That this long but most interesting route presents many difficulties to the bicyclist we do not conceal; but it *is* practicable. Most riders, however, will no doubt be glad of occasional "lifts" among the Welsh hills, where immense sums of money have nevertheless been spent in road-making, and great engineering difficulties overcome. There is a shorter route, but it can only be used at the expense of missing many interesting spots.

OBJECTS OF INTEREST.

A volume might be written about the attractiveness of this route, and whether the tourist's proclivities be in the direction of industrial centres, engineering enterprise, ecclesiastical æsthetics, or landscapes of every possible variety of loveliness, he will be abundantly satisfied with this trip.

WOLVERHAMPTON.—The Sun Bicycle Club, Sun Inn, Commercial Road.

BIRMINGHAM.—*The Steel Pen Manufactory of Messrs. Gillott; the *Electro-Plate Works of Messrs. Elkington ; and the *Small Arms Factory at Smallheath.

LLANGOLLEN.—On a conical hill, not far from the town, are the ruins of Cadr Dinas Brau, a castle of great antiquity.

BETTWS-Y-COED.—*The Swallow Falls.

CAPEL CERRIG.—The ascent of Snowden may be made here.

BANGOR.—**The Britannia Tube. **The Menai Bridge. Circular tours throughout the whole of North Wales may be arranged here. The "George," at the Menai Bridge, overlooking the Straits, will be found a most comfortable head-quarters.

HOLYHEAD.—*The Stack Lighthouse.

HOTELS.

*Birmingham—*Great Western, Hen and Chickens*. Wednesbury—*Dartmouth Arms, Red Lion*. Shiffnall—*Jerningham Arms, Star*. Wolverhampton—*The Swan*. Shrewsbury—*The Lion, The Raven, The George*. Oswestry—*The Wynnstay Arms*. Llangollen—*The Hand, Royal*. Corwen—*Owen Glendwr*. Bettws-y-Coed—*Royal Oak, Waterloo*. Bangor—*Penrhyn Arms*. Menai Bridge —*The George*. Holyhead—*The Royal*.

Route IV.

LONDON TO YORK.

LONDON to Norman's Cross (see Route I.), 75¾ miles ; Kate's Cabin Inn, 79¼ ; STAMFORD, 89 ; Greetham, 97 ; GRANTHAM, 110 ; Shire Bridge, 120¼ ; NEWARK, 124 ; Cromwell, 129¾ ; TUXFORD, 137½ ; EAST RETFORD, 144¾ ; Bawtry, 153 ; Rossington Bridge, 157½ ; DONCASTER, 162 ; Robin Hood's Well, 169 ; Went Bridge, 172½ ; Darrington, 174¼ ; Brotherton, 178¼ ; South Milford, 182 ; Tadcaster, 190¼ ; YORK, 199¼.

NOTES ON THE ROADS.

There are some unpleasant bits of road in the neighbourhood of Doncaster on the Tadcaster side; and in wet weather the last part of the route will be, undoubtedly, the worst. The soil is stiff clay, and is described by an expert as "quite impassable for bicycles," progress being impossible until the foot-path was resorted to. Some parts of the road are, however, as good as any in England.

OBJECTS OF INTEREST.

NEWARK.—Ruins of the Old Castle.

YORK.—**The Cathedral, All Saints', St. Mary's, and St. Margaret Churches. *The Castle, *The Guildhall, *The ancient Walls of the town.

HOTELS.

Stamford—*Stamford Arms, George.* Grantham—*Angel, George.* Newark—*Clinton Arms, Ram.* Tuxford—*Newcastle Arms, Sun.* East Retford—*White Hart.* Bawtry—*Crown, Bull.* Doncaster—*Angel, Old George.* York—*Black Swan, Harker's.*

Route V.

LONDON TO CHESTER.

LONDON to DUNSTABLE (see Route II.), 33½ miles; Hockliffe, 37¼; WOBURN, 41½; NEWPORT PAGNELL, 50; Horton Inn, 58½; NORTHAMPTON, 66; Creaton, 73¾; North Kilworth, 83¾; LUTTERWORTH, 89; High Cross, 95; Hinckley, 99½; ATHERSTONE, 107½; TAMWORTH, 115⅞; LICHFIELD, 23½; RUGELEY, 131; STAFFORD, 140¾; ECCLESHALL, 147¾; Dormoton, 159½; BRIDGEMORE, 162¼; Nantwich, 169¼; TARPORLEY, 178¼; Stanford Bridge, 184; CHESTER, 188½.

NOTES ON THE ROAD.

Universal testimony is in favour of the condition of the roadway on this route; and deviations from it enable the traveller to see Derbyshire. At High Cross, two Roman roads cross—the Fosse and Watling Street. From this point a run of 12½ miles brings us to Leicester, whence to Lancaster there is a route we shall describe in its place. Market Harborough, Ashby-de-la-Zouch, and Melton Mowbray can also be reached by divergence from Route V. at High Cross, and the Leicestershire roads are proverbially excellent.

OBJECTS OF INTEREST.

This route passes through a district where many of the staple industries of this country are carried on, and opulence appears to prevail. The limits of this work do not admit of detailed reference to the magnificent scenery of the Peak, Matlock, and Bakewell, or the glories of Haddon Hall, or of Chatsworth. However, there are guide-books galore to instruct the tourist; and the Derbyshire roads present no difficulties if the bicyclist keeps to the valleys. The geological condition of the county is favourable for road-making generally.

WOBURN.—**About a mile from the town is Woburn Abbey, the splendid seat of the Duke of Bedford.

NORTHAMPTON.—The True Briton Bicycle Club, Maple Street. The Northampton Star Bicycle Club, Cross Key's Hotel, Sheep Street.

TAMWORTH.—The *Castle. Near the town the residence of the Peel family.

LICHFIELD.—*Cathedral. The free Grammar School, at which were educated Addison, Woolaston, Ashmole, Garrick, and Johnson.

STAFFORD.—The house in which Isaac Walton was born.

NANTWICH.—*The Salt Quarries.

CHESTER.—The quaintest and most interesting town in England. **The "Row," **God's Providence House. The Walls. The Cathedral. **Eaton Hall, the magnificent seat of the Marquis of Westminster.

HOTELS.

Woburn.—*Bedford Arms.* Newport Pagnell—*Anchor, Swan.* *Northampton, —*George.* Hinckley—*George.* Atherstone—*Red Lion, Angel.* Tamworth—*Castle, *Peel Arms.* Lichfield—*Swan, George, Old Crown, Three Crowns.* Stafford—*North Western, *Swan.* Nantwich—*Lamb, Crown.* Chester—*Grosvenor, *Queen.*

Route VI.

LONDON TO BATH.

(This Route is measured from Hyde Park Corner.)

LONDON to Kensington, 1½; Turnham Green, 5; BRENTFORD, 7; HOUNSLOW, 9¾; Colnbrook, 17¼; Slough, 20½; MAIDENHEAD, 26; Twyford, 34; Reading, 39; Puntifield, 45; Woolhampton, 49¼; Speenham Land, 56; HUNGERFORD, 64½; Froxfield, 67½; Cross Ford, 69; Marlborough, 74½; Beckhampton, 81¼; DEVIZES, 88¾; Summerham Bridge, 91¾; Shaw, 97¾; Kingsdown Hill, 103; Bath Easton, 104¾; BATH, 107¼.

NOTES ON THE ROAD.

This is a favourite route with bicyclists. The return journey is preferred if speed be an object; although there is an almost impossible hill to mount on the London side of Marlborough, on the homeward journey, and some of the Berkshire highways are sandy. From Newbury to London the route is fairly level.

OBJECTS OF INTEREST,

Berkshire presents a fine bold country, and Windsor and the Vale of the White Horse can be visited by easy deviations from the route. The open wild country roads of Wiltshire have long been favourites with pedestrian tourists, and there is no part of England richer in Druidical remains, all of which can be reached by cross roads in connection with this route.

BATH.—The **Abbey and the fine Church of St. Michael. The view from Beacon Hill.

HOTELS.

Brentford—*Royal.* Slough—**Crown.* Maidenhead—*White Hart, Bear, Skindle's.* Twyford—*Station Hotel, King's Arms.* Reading—*Great Western, George.* Hungerford—*Black Bear.* Marlborough—*Aylesbury Arms.* Devizes—*Bear, Castle.* Bath—*The York House, White Hart, The Grand.*

Route VII.

BATH TO NOTTINGHAM.

From BATH to Dunkirk, 15; Tetbury, 22; Bridge over Thames and Severn Canal, 28¾; CIRENCESTER, 32¼; Foss Cross, 38¼; Broadwater Flats, 45¼;

Stow Bridge, 47½; STOW-ON-THE-WOLD, 51¼; MORETON-IN-THE-MARSH, 55½; Halford Bridge, 65¾; Upper Eatington, 68¼; Wellesburne Hastang, 12¾; WARWICK, 72½; KENILWORTH, 84¾; COVENTRY, 89¾ (see Route II); NUN-EATON, 98¼; HINCKLEY, 103½ (see Route V); LEICESTER, 116½; LOUGHBOROUGH, 127½; NOTTINGHAM, 142½.

NOTES ON THE ROAD.

This is neither the longest nor the shortest route that might be adopted, but we have chosen it because the turnpike roads are of average excellence, and the route is divisable into an easy two day's work by breaking the journey at Warwick,—about 80 miles per diem being a fair day's distance for a competent bicyclist.

OBJECTS OF INTEREST.

**Warwick Castle, *Guy's Cliff, and Kenilworth. From Warwick it is only a run of 8 miles to **Stratford-on-Avon (Shakspeare's).

NOTTINGHAM.—The Castle, Market Place, and the large Hosiery and Lace Factories.

LEICESTER.—**Splendid Roman remains, and very old ruins of the Abbey, where Wolsey came " to lay his bones."

DUNKIRK.—**Badminton Park, the seat of the Duke of Beaufort.

CIRENCESTER.— Grismond's Tower, Alfred's Hall, where King Alfred signed the treaty with Guthrum, the Dane.

HOTELS.

Tetbury—*Talbot, White Hart.* Cirencester—*King's Head, Ram.* Moreton-in-the-Marsh—*Unicorn.* Warwick—*Warwick Arms, *Woolpack.* Kenilworth—*King's Arms.* Nuneaton—*Ball, Newdegate Arms.* Leicester—**Bell, Stag and. Pheasant.* Loughboro'—*King's Head, *Bull.* Nottingham—**George, *Lion.* Stratford—**Red Horse, Shakespeare.*

Route VIII.

NOTTINGHAM TO CAMBRIDGE.

From NOTTINGHAM to Bunny, 7 miles; LOUGHBOROUGH, 15; LEICESTER, 24, MARKET HARBOROUGH, 38½; KETTERING, 56¼; HUNTINGDON, 72; CAMBRIDGE,

NOTES ON THE ROAD.

The mingling of loose gravel with granite makes the road from Nottingham to Loughborough undesirable. Otherwise there is a good level road the whole way, except a few steep but short gradients between Market Harborough and Kettering.

OBJECTS OF INTEREST.

There is little to detain the rider on this route. Pretty, rural scenery abounds, but it is emphatically a road for doing good time on, and the emulous bicyclist may endeavour, if he likes, to outstrip the winner of the Oxford and Cambridge Bicycle Race of 1874, on a rapid journey over this course. His actual time was 9h. 10m.

CAMBRIDGE.—**The College.   **King's College Chapel.   **Cambridge University Bicycle Club.**

HOTELS-

Market Harborough—*Angel.*   Kettering—*George.*   Huntingdon—*George, Fountain.* Cambridge—*Hoop, Bull.*

Route IX.

OXFORD TO CAMBRIDGE.

From OXFORD to Headington, 2 miles; Wheatley, 6½; THAME, 31; AYLESBURY, 32¾; Beacon Hill, 33¾; DUNSTABLE, 38¾ (see Route II); Hitchin, 34 (see Route I); BALDOCK, 59; ROYSTON, 67; CAMBRIDGE, 82¼.

NOTES ON THE ROAD.

This is the course over which the Inter-University match was run, in 1874, and is a fair road. The distance is roundly stated to be 84 miles in the report of the race, but we cannot, from the best authorities at our disposal, add to our figures anent the matter.

OBJECTS OF INTEREST.

OXFORD.—**The College Chapels.   *The Cathedral.   **Blenheim Park and Woodstock, the hereditary seat of the Dukes of Marlborough. Ely, 16 miles from Cambridge. **The Cathedral and ancient houses. **The Dark Blue Bicycle Club, 24, New Inn, Hall Street.**

HOTELS.

Oxford—*Clarendon, *Randolph.*   Thame—*Spread Eagle.*   Baldock—*Rose and Crown.* Royston—*Bull.*

Route X.

LONDON TO THE LAKE DISTRICT.

Fom LONDON to DUNSTABLE, 33½ (see Route I and II); HOCKLIFFE, 37¼; WOBURN, 41½; Wavendon, 45; NEWPORT PAGNELL, 50; Stoke Goldington, 54½; Hackleton, 60; NORTHAMPTON, 66: Kingsthorpe, 67½; MARKET HARBOROUGH, 83½; Kibworth, 89; Oadby, 94½; LEICESTER, 98; MOUNTSORREL, 105; LOUGHBOROUGH, 109; Shardlow, 119½; DERBY, 126; Brailsford, 133; Ashbourn, 139¼; Hanging Bridge, 141; LEEK, 154¼; Hog Bridge, 160¼; Bosley, 161¾; MACCLESFIELD, 167¼; Bullock Smithy, 176½; Stockport, 179¼; Manchester, 186; Middle Hulton, 197; Blackrode, 203¼; Chorley, 208¼; PRESTON, 217½; Bilsborough, 224½; Garstang, 228¾; Galgate Bridge, 235½; LANCASTER, 240; Bolton-le-Sands, 244; Burton, 251; KENDAL, 261¾; Bowness, 271½.

NOTES ON THE ROAD.

On leaving Leek, the tourist must avoid going through Wilmslow by the Alderley road, as round stones are used for paving it, and go by Chelford. The approach to Chorley is also rough, but improves in the neighbourhood of Garstang, through Preston. From Kendal to Bowness there is ten miles of rough work, and after that the bicycle must be supplemented by other modes of travel, if the district is to be explored thoroughly.

OBJECTS OF INTEREST.

Apart from the well-known beauties of Windermere, Keswick, Furness, &c , there is very fine scenery, with many interesting spots on the road. Manchester, Lancaster, &c., offer varied attractions, and will no doubt induce the tourist to halt frequently. A good map is very useful on this route, but *not* the Ordnance.

MACCLESFIELD.—Ancient Grammar School.

HOTELS.

Derby—*Royal, Midland.* Macclesfield—*Angel.* Stockport—*George, Commercial.* Chorley—*Royal Oak, Leigh Arms.* Garstang—*Royal Oak.* Lancaster—*King's Arms, Royal Hotel.* Kendal—*King's Arms, *Crown.* Manchester—*County Palatine, Queen's.* Preston—*Victoria.* Furness—*Abbey.* Bowness—*Royal, Crown, Old England, Prince of Wales.* Lancaster—*King's Arms, County, Feathers.*

Route XI.

LONDON TO EXETER.

From LONDON to HOUNSLOW, 9¾ miles (see Route XVI.); Bedfont, 13¼ STAINES, 16½; Virginia Water, 20½; Bagshot, 26; Hartley Row, 36¼; Hook, 39¼; Basingstoke, 45¼; Worting, 47½; WHITCHURCH, 56½; ANDOVER, 63½; Winterslow Hutt, 75; SALISBURY, 81½; Combe Bisset or Basset, 84¼; Woodyates Inn, 91¼; Pimperne, 101¼; BLANDFORD, 103½; Winterborne Whitchurch, 108¾; DORCHESTER, 119½; Winterborne Abbas, 124½; BRIDPORT, 134¾; Charmouth, 141½; AXMINSTER, 146¾; Kilmington, 148¼; Wilmington, 152¾; HONITON, 156½; Rockbere, 166¾; EXETER, 173.

NOTES ON THE ROAD.

That this route presents serious difficulties to the bicyclist cannot be denied, and an average rate of speed is scarcely attainable all through. However, no tourist will ever be content without seeing South Devon, and as the road, for at least two-thirds of the way, is easily traversable, he will find that *le jeu vaut la chandelle* so far as we have taken him in this instance.

OBJECTS OF INTEREST

**Virginia Water. **Windsor Castle, 7 miles distant through the Great Park. At Old Basing, near Mapledurwell Hatch, the ruins of Basing House, defended by the Marquis of Winchester against the Parliamentary forces.

Salisbury.—The **Cathedral, with its magnificent north front.   Druidical Circle at Stonehenge adjacent, *via* Amesbury,

Dorchester.—Roman remains.   From this town Weymouth and the Isle of Portland can be easily visited.

Axminster—**Carpet Factories.

Exeter.—The ancient **Cathedral.   Ruins of Rougemont Castle.

HOTELS.

Staines—*Angel and Crown.*   Virginia Water—*Wheatsheaf.*   Basingstoke— *Red Lion, *Wheatsheaf.*   Whitchurch—*White Hart, King's Arms.*   Andover— *Star and Garter.*   Salisbury—*Three Swans, White Hart.*   Blandford—*Crown.* Dorchester—*King's Arms, Antelope.*   Bridport—*Bull.*   Axminster—*George. Bell.*   Honiton—*Dolphin, Lion.*   Exeter—*Pople's New London, Half-Moon.*

Route XII.

LONDON TO BIDEFORD.

From London to Exeter, 173 miles (see Route XI) ; Cowley Bridge, 175 ; Newton St. Cyres, 177½ ; Crediton, 180½ ; Bow, 188 ; North Tawton, 192 ; Exborn, 196¼ ; Hatherleigh, 201 ; Torrington, 211½ ; Bideford, 218.

NOTES ON THE ROADS.

In proportion as the beauties of the road increase, so do the difficulties of Devonshire travel.   In wet weather the tourist is most certain to find bicycling unsatisfactory to the last degree in this county.

OBJECTS OF INTEREST.

Bideford and its adjacent towns are deservedly popular with tourists ; the climate being less enervating than that of South Devon, and greater interest attaching to the coast scenery.   Ilfracombe, Westward Hoe, and Clovelly, can be reached from here.

HOTELS.

Crediton—*Ship.*   Hatherleigh—*George, London.*   Bideford—*Commercial, New Inn.*

Route XIII.

LONDON TO THE LAND'S END.

London to Exeter, 173 miles (see Route XI); Lilly Bridge, 179¼ ; Crockernwell, 184 ; Stickle Path, 191¾ ; Okehampton, 195¼ ; Bridestow, 201¼ ; Lyfton, 210¼ , Launceston, 213¾ ; Hick's Mill, 218¾ ; Five Lanes Inn, 221½ ; Temple, 228¾ , Bodmin, 234¾ ; East Lane End, 241¼ ; St. Michael, 249¾ ; Truro, 256¾ ; Perranwell, 261¼ ; Trewannock, 272¼ ; Helstone, 273¾.; Marazion, 282¾ ; Penzance, 286¾ ; Trebear, 294¼ ; Trevescan, 297 ; Land's End, 297¾.

NOTES ON THE ROADS.

It is certain that none but the most enterprising and robust bicyclists will get through this route, and frequent dismounts must be made.   Nevertheless it is worth a trial if the rider does not mind rough work.   He should bear in mind that Cornwall is very badly supplied with accommodation for travellers, and need not imagine that at every village he arrives at he will find what he requires; indeed a friend of ours applied at a house with a public-house signboard suspended in front of it, near Helstone, and was naïvely told he could not have any beer, but that they were thinking about brewing next week, and he could have either hard cider or butter milk.

OBJECTS OF INTEREST

Are numerous in the vicinity of this route, and we strongly advise plenty of time to be given to it, and several détours to be made.   Teignmouth, Dawlish, and Torquay should be visited, the valley of the Dart descended, and Plymouth is to be reached by a deviation at Okehampton, viâ Tavistock, at a distance of 15 miles ; Plymouth, 29.

HOTELS.

Okehampton—*White Hart.*   Launceston—*White Hart, King's Arms.* Bodmin—*Oliver's, Town Arms,* Truro—*Red Lion, Royal.* Helstone—*Angel, Globe.*—Penzance—*Queen's, Union.*   Land's End—*The First and Last Inn in England.*   Plymouth—**Royal, Duke of Cornwall.*

Route XIV.

LONDON TO BRIGHTON.

From LONDON to Brixton, 3¼ miles ; CROYDON, 9¼ ; Marden Park, 15¼ ; Godstone Green, 19 ; East Grinstead, 28½ ; Wych Cross, 34 ; Nutley, 37 ; Maresfield, 39¾ ; Uckfield, 41½ ; Horstead, 43½ ; Cliff, 49½ ; LEWES Town Hall, 50 ; Falmer, 54 ; BRIGHTON, 58¼.

OBJECTS OF INTEREST.

LEWES.—The *Castle and Museum.

HOTELS.

Croydon—*Greyhound.* East Grinstead—*Dorset Amrs.* Maresfield—*Chequers.* Lewes—*White Hart, Star.*

Route XV.

LONDON TO BRIGHTON.

From LONDON to CROYDON, 9¼ miles (see Route XIV) ; Foxley Hatch, 12 ; Merstham, 17¾ ; Red Hill, 20½ ; Horley, 24 ; CRAWLEY, 29 ; Staplefield Common, 34¾ ; Hicksted, 40 ; Piecombe, 45¼ ; BRIGHTON, 51½.

NOTES ON THE ROADS.

Of these two routes, the latter is preferred for coaching purposes, Crawley being the half-way house. A bicyclist writes to the *Field* and says he cannot understand the Brighton route's popularity, as there are numerous severe slopes. This is true, but there is no better road out of London than the Croydon road, except, perhaps, the Clapham route through Tooting (Upper), 5¼ miles from London; Sutton, 11¼; Obelisk, Banstead Downs, 13; REIGATE, 21; and Crawley, where route XV. can be taken up. The choice of three routes enables the tourist to vary the journey out and home.

OBJECTS OF INTEREST.

BRIGHTON.—The **Aquarium; the two *Piers; the *Pavilion; and the Devil's Dyke. The Brighton Bicycle Club, 14, Queen's Road.

HOTELS.

Sutton—*The Cock Inn.* Red Hill—*Railway.* Horley—*King's Head.* Crawley—*George.* Reigate—*White Hart, Swan.* Brighton—*The *New Ship, The Grand, The Bedford, The Old Ship, The Albion.*

Route XVI.

LONDON TO SOUTHAMPTON.

(Distance measured from Hyde Park Corner.)

From London to Hounslow, 9¾ miles (see Route XI.); STAINES, 16⅓; (or by Kingston, Hampton, and the Thames Valley, two miles farther, and a much more enjoyable route); Virginia Water, 20½; Golden Farmer, 27½; Farnborough, 32; FARNHAM, 38¼; Froyle; 44½; Alton, 47½; Ropley Dean, 54¾; ALRESFORD, 57¼; WINCHESTER, 65; Chandler's Ford Bridge, 71½; SOUTHAMPTON, 77.

NOTES ON THE ROADS.

There are some tremendous slopes in some parts of this route, nevertheless a vigorous bicyclist has actually attempted the Isle of Wight after completing it. We advise none of our readers to cross the Solent, as there is no level riding at all in the best parts of Vectis. The return route may be varied by going across Netley Heath, and through Titchfield and Fareham to Gosport, leaving the main road at its entrance into Southampton. On the other hand the New Forest can be easily reached viâ Eling, Lyndhurst, and so on to Lymington, nearly 90 miles from London. The roads are fair throughout the greater parts of Surrey, Berks, and North Hants.

OBJECTS OF INTEREST.

If the tourist is still "asking for more" after seeing the old City and Cathedral of Winchester, Holy Cross Abbey, the roadside scenery, and Netley Abbey on this route, he can deviate at Farnham, and 10 miles will bring him to Guildford, and thence viâ Albury, there is Dorking within easy reach, and the adjacent range of hillsnear, which are not nearly well enough known to Londoners. The view from St. Martha's hill—which however cannot be ascended on a bicycle—down the vale of Albury, is very beautiful.

WINCHESTER.—Ancient *Cathedral and City. The College, founded by Bishop Wykeham in 1390.

SOUTHAMPTON.—**Netley Abbey, &c.

HOTELS.

Staines—*Angel and Crown.* Virginia Water—**Wheatsheaf.* Farnham—*Bush, Lion and Lamb.* Alton—*Swan, Crown.* Alresford—*Swan, Horse and Groom.* Winchester—*The George, Black Swan.* Southampton—**South Western, *Radley's, Dolphin, Royal.* Titchfield—*Bugle.* Fareham—*Red Lion.* Gosport—*India Arms, Star.* Lymington—*Nag's Head, Angel.*

Route XVII.

LONDON TO HASTINGS.

(Distance measured from London Bridge, Surrey side.)

From London Bridge to Lewisham (viâ New Cross), 5 miles ; Bromley, 10 ; Farnborough, 14 ; Sevenoaks, 23½ ; Watt's Cross, 27¼ ; TUNBRIDGE, 30 ; Tunbridge Wells, 35¾ ; Wadhurst, 42¼ ; Hurst Green, 48½ ; Robertsbridge, 51 ; HASTINGS, 64½.

NOTES ON THE ROADS.

There are no serious impediments to the bicycle rider on this journey, a proof of which is that it has become a favorite road for amateurs in four-in-hand driving.

OBJECTS OF INTEREST.

The lovely scenery around Tunbridge Wells renders this as attractive as any route out of London, and it has the additional advantage of having a pleasant termination at so popular a marine resort as Hastings, a centre for many pleasant runs.

TUNBRIDGE.—The Church ; the Wells ; and the ruins of the Castle.

HOTELS.

Bromley—*White Hart.* Sevenoaks—*Royal Crown, Royal Oak.* Tunbridge—*Rose and Crown.* Tunbridge Wells—*The Calverley, *Kentish Royal, Royal Sussex.* Wadhurst—*Railway.* Hurst Green—*George.* Robertsbridge—*Old George, Ostrich.* Hastings—*Queen's, *The Marine, Albion, Castle, Warrior, Montague's, Green's.*

Route XVIII.

BRIGHTON TO TUNBRIDGE WELLS.

From BRIGHTON to LEWES (see Route XIV) 8¼ ; Horstead, 14¾ ; Cooper's Green, 18 ; Crowborough Mill, 24 ; Hamsell Bridge, 27 ; TUNBRIDGE WELLS, 31.

NOTES OF THE ROADS.

On this short but pleasant route, there is nothing to puzzle the bicyclist but the slopes outside Brighton, which have not deterred many from facing them twice a day, on the Brighton and back tour of 102 miles or so.

OBJECTS OF INTEREST.

The quaint old town of Lewes will possibly be again made a halting place. It is full of historical associations of great antiquity. Newhaven is 10 miles from Lewes

HOTELS.

Lewes—*Star, * White Hart.*   Newhaven—*London and Paris.*

Route XIX.

BRIGHTON TO MARGATE.

From BRIGHTON to LEWES, (see Route XVIII) 8¼ miles ; Ringmer, 10¾ ; Eason's Green, 16 ; Heathfield Tower Hill, 22 ; Burwash, 28 ; Hurst Green, 32 ; Highgate, 35½ ; Hartley Street, 38 ; CRANBROOK, 40 ; Wilsley Green, 41 ; Standen, 46 ; Pluckley, 53¼ ; Challock Lees, 60¼ ; Shalmsford Street, 66 ; CANTERBURY, 70 ; MARGATE, 86¼.

NOTES ON THE ROADS.

The Kentish roads are as a rule good.

OBJECTS OF INTEREST

Are not numerous on this route, except the tourist (which is generally the case), is satisfied with a close inspection of Thomas á Becket's Cathedral and the antiquities of Canterbury, or enjoys a few days stay in the three ever-popular watering places of the Isle of Thanet.

HOTELS.

Ringmer—*Anchor.*   Heathfield—*Crown.*   Burwash—*Admiral Vernon,* Cranbrook—*Bull, George.* Pluckley—*Dering Arms.* Canterbury—*Rose, Fountain, Fleur-de-Lis.*   Margate—**Cliftonville, White Hart, *York.*

Route XX.

LONDON TO FOLKESTONE.

From LONDON to Blackheath, 5 miles (viâ New Cross) ; Shooter's Hill, 8 ; Crayford, 13 ; DARTFORD, 15 ; Galley Hill, 19 ; GRAVESEND, 22 ; ROCHESTER, 29 ; Rainham, 34 ; Sittingbourne, 40 ; Ospringe, 46 ; Harbledown, 54 ; CANTERBURY, 55¼ (see Route XIX) ; Bridge (over R. Stour,) 58½ ; Half-way House, 63½ ; Ewell, 68 ; DOVER, 71 ; FOLKESTONE, 77½.

NOTES ON THE ROADS.

There are numerous gradients on this route, but they are not insurmountable, and the rider will probably be well advised to avail himself of the railway for the last six miles.

OBJECTS OF INTEREST.

This route is full of interest and is capable of easy extension to many quaint old Kentish towns on the coast, such as Hythe, Sandwich, and Rye. Saltwood Castle and Shorncliffe Camp can be reached from Folkestone, the roads thence being good if not very level.

Rochester.—**Cathedral and ruins of Castle.   **Fortifications of Chatham.
Dover.—**The Castle,
Folkestone.—Shorncliffe Camp.   Saltwood Castle.

HOTELS.

Blackheath—*Crown.* Dartford—*Bull, King's Head.* Gravesend—*New Falcon, Old Falcon.*   Rochester—*Victoria, Bull, Crown*   Rainham—*White Horse.* Sittingbourne—*Bull, Lion.*   Dover—*Lord Warden, Ship, *Harp, Dover Castle.* Folkestone—*Pavilion, Clarendon, West Cliff.*

Route XXI.

LONDON TO NORWICH.

(Distances measured from Whitechapel Church.)

From London to Bow, 2½ miles ; Snaresbrook, 6¾ ; Woodford Wells, 9 ; Epping, 16¾ ; Harlow, 23¼ ; Spel Brook, 27½ ; Stanstead, 32¾ ; Newport, 38½ ; Great Chesterford, 44¾ ; Bourn Bridge, 49¼ ; Worsted Lodge (Junction with Roman Road), 50¼ ; Devil's Ditch, 59 ; Newmarket, 60¾ ; Red House, 66¼ ; Barton Mills, 69¼ ; Elvedon, 76¼ ;. Thetford, 80 ; Larling Heath, 87¼ ; Attleborough, 94 ; Wymondham or Wyndham, 100 ; Easton, 106½ ; Norwich, 108½.

NOTES ON THE ROADS.

The reputation of the old "Eastern Counties" Railway not being of the best, we are glad to be able to testify to the general excellence of the coach roads in that region.   Eastern routes have not hitherto being favorites with bicyclists, but there is no reason why they should not become so.

OBJECTS OF INTEREST.

Norwich—The Cathedral ; the Castle, a fine specimen of Norman Architecture ; fine Market Place, and splendid Church of St. Peter's Mancroft.

HOTELS.

Harlow—*George, Green Man.*   Newmarket—*White Hart, Rutland Arms.* Thetford—*Bell, Anchor.*   Attleborough—*New.*   Wymondham—*Queen's Head, King's Head, Norwich.*

Route XXII.

LONDON TO IPSWICH.

(Distances measured as in previous Route).

From London to Stratford, 3½ miles ;   Ilford Bridge, 6¾ ;   Romford, 11¾ ; Brentwood, 18 ; Ingatestone, 23 ; Chelmsford, 29 ; Witham, 37¾ ; Kelvedon, 41 ; Colchester, 50¾ ; Stratford Bridge, 58¼ ; Copdock, 65¼ ; Ipswich, 69.

NOTES ON THE ROADS.

Ipswich is reached by this route at Stone's End, and the route can be extended to Norwich, by Coddenham Bridge (27¼), passing Eye on the left near Thwaite, and Diss on the right, at Osmuldestone. This road to Norwich is, however, some few miles longer than that indicated in Route XXI.

OBJECTS OF INTEREST.

COLCHESTER—The Castle, St. John's Abbey, and other antiquities. Adjacent scenery of the Coln.

HOTELS.

Romford—*White Hart, Golden Lion.* Brentwood—*White Hart, George.* Chelmsford—*Saracen's Head, White Hart, Bell.* Witham—*White Hart, Eagle.* Kelvedon—*Star and Fleece.* Colchester—*Three Cups, Red Lion, George.* Ipswich—*White Horse, Crown and Anchor.*

Route XXIII.

CAMBRIDGE TO HARWICH.

From CAMBRIDGE to NEWMARKET, 13 miles ; Kentford Bridge, 18 ; Saxham, 23 ; BURY ST. EDMUNDS, 27 ; Beighton, 23½ ; STOW MARKET, 42¼ ; Needham, 44 ; IPSWICH, 52½ (see Route XXII) ; Brantham Church, 60½ ; MANNINGTREE, 63½ ; HARWICH, 75.

NOTES ON THE ROADS.

Although this road is not as level as others in the Eastern Counties that we have given, there are no serious difficulties thereon for a bicycle rider of fair ability.

OBJECTS OF INTEREST.

BURY ST. EDMUNDS—**Hengrave Hall, an interesting show house. Walton-on-the-Naze, and Dovercourt adjacent.

HOTELS.

Bury St. Edmund's—*Angel, Bell, Suffolk.* Stowmarket—*King's Head, Fox.* Needham—*Swan.* Manningtree—*White Hart, Packet.* Harwich—*Great Eastern, Three Cups.*

Route XXIV.

LONDON TO YARMOUTH.

(Distances measured from Whitechapel Church.)

From LONDON to IPSWICH (see Route XXII), 69 miles ; WOODBRIDGE, 76¾ ; Wickham Market, 81½ ; Stratford St. Andrew, 86¼ ; SAXMUNDHAM, 89½ ; Yoxford, 93¾ ; Blythburgh, 99¼ ; Wangford, 102¼ ; Wrentham, 106 ; Lowestoft, 114 ; South Town, 122¾ ; YARMOUTH, 124.

NOTES ON THE ROADS.

There is no road for a hundred odd miles' stretch out of London, with so much dead level as this. There is another route, omitting Lowestoft, viâ Henham Park, Brampton, Shaddingfield, Weston and Beccles ; and still another viâ Harleston and Bungay. In the latter case the distance is augmented by about three miles.

OBJECTS OF INTEREST.

YARMOUTH—St. Nicholas Church, with its fine Organ; the Quay, Shipping, and Fisheries.

HOTELS.

Woodbridge—*Crown.* Lowestoft—*Royal, Crown, Suffolk.* Yarmouth—*Victoria, Royal, Angel, Bath.* Saxmundham—*Bell, White Hart.*

Route XXV.

LONDON TO CROMER.

(*Distances measured from Whitechapel Church.*)

From London to NORWICH (see Route XXI), 108½; Crostwick, 113¼; Horstead, 115¼; Westwick Hall Park, 119½; NORTH WALSHAM, 122¾; Antingham, 125¼; CROMER, 131¾.

NOTES ON THE ROADS.

There is an absence of bicycle experience on record as to this as well as other Eastern Counties' routes. The roads offer no impediment of any importance, to a rider of a bicycle of fairly good construction.

OBJECTS OF INTEREST.

CROMER—The Bay, the Sands, and the remains of the old Church, 14th century architecture.

Cromer—*Tucker's, Belle Vue, Hotel de Paris.* North Walsham—*King's Arms.*

The following routes have the practical advantage of having been traversed by Bicyclists, and the information given is the result of their experience, and consequently will be found strictly reliable.

STAMFORD to GRANTHAM.—Cottersworth to Grantham is a good hard road, with a slight rise towards the latter end; after Grantham, there is a steep hill at Great Gonerby, which requires stiff work, followed by a splendid run to Newark of about 12 miles; thence through Muskham, Carlton, Tuxford, to Retford. The roads are good, with only one steep hill.

CIRENCESTER to SALISBURY, about 66 miles, *via* Malmesbury, Chippenham, Calne, Melksham, Westbury, and Warminster. The first 4½ miles consist of Roman Road white stone, hilly, rutty and rough, and when wet, very greasy; thence through Malmesbury to Calne, 20½ miles, the road is grey and yellow stone, good surface, undulating, with one big hill just before Calne. Calne to Melksham, 8 miles, same stone, very rough, and undulating. Melksham to Warminster, 12 miles, same stone, gradually improving to an asphalt-like smoothness at Warminster, near to which there are two good hills. Warminster to Salisbury, 22 miles, good flint surface, very undulating but levels favorable.

Marlborough to Salisbury, 37 miles, *via* Abury to Devizes, latter part hilly, rough, and very exposed.

Devizes to Salisbury, *via* Upavon and Amesbury, 25 miles. The road is undulating, with flint surface, but affords good running to Amesbury, then take the upper road to the left, this is hilly but the best, particularly in wet weather.

Marlborough to Salisbury, 28 miles, *via* Collingbourns, Cholderton, and Parton. There is a good flint road for the first 8 miles, then after you get clear of Kennet valley, the gradients will be found to be easy and the surface fair. Thence a disused piece 15 miles long. Keep left to the Collingbourns and the road will keep good; thence to Cholderton, 12 miles. From Salisbury the road is undulating but good.

Basingstoke to Salisbury, 35 miles, *via* Whitchurch and Andover. To the distance of the 71st mile from London the road will be found good, with flint surface, and undulating. There are four or five very rough hills.

Winchester to Salisbury, 23 miles, *via* Stockbridge. This is a very bad road, being rough, hilly, and much exposed. One of the hills being $1\frac{1}{2}$ miles long.

Winchester to Salisbury, 26 miles, *via* Romsey. The first five miles are chiefly gravel; to Hursley, flint surface, hilly and rather rough. The surface gradually improves. From Romsey, there is half-a-mile up hill, smooth but steep. Then another down, not steep but rough; then the road undulates for 6 miles, good on the whole, the exception being a few odd patches. Seven miles from Salisbury you come to an ascent of two miles, steep only in short bits. After this there is a splendid run to Salisbury, downhill almost all the way.

Salisbury to Southampton. Road all gravel, with good surface, though tending to be hilly in portions.

Salisbury to Christchurch, *via* Fordingbridge, 26 miles. The road is nearly all gravel, and after the first 3 miles almost a deal level, with a good surface, but in portions inclined to be sandy.—Salisbury to Blandford, 23 miles. This road is of a flat surface over the Downs, and is very rough and hilly.—Salisbury to Shaftesbury, 20 miles. The road runs through Wilton, Barford, and Forant. The surface is all flint, except close to Shaftesbury, but good all the way. It is nearly level to Barford, but hilly after.

N.B.—The road marked as going direct to Bruton *via* Stourhead, leaving at the 19th mile from Salisbury, is barely visible as a grass track

Southampton to Warminster (64 miles), *via* Cadnom Bridge, Ringwood, Blandford, and Shaftesbury. As far as Wimborne (28 miles) gravel extends. After the first eight miles there is a long ascent, but not steep, about a mile; then the road undulates, and there is a long down hill to Ringwood. The surface is loose on the hills. Ringwood to Wimborne the road is level, but sandy here and there. Wimborne to Shaftesbury is 21 miles, and the surface of the road good. Avoid the upper and right-hand road, as it is hilly and rough; take the lower, which leads you well till within two miles of Shaftesbury, and then you have a steep bit up and down. From Shaftesbury for 15 miles the roads are decidedly hilly, and the middle six miles are stoney and rough. Two miles from Shaftesbury there is a steep zigzag descent, three-quarters of a mile long, then several stiffish ascents in the next eight miles. Now a good run down of a mile, and a capital road into Warminster.

NOTES ON THE ROADS IN WILTS, HANTS, AND DORSET.—These roads are not really level, except near Southampton, Ringwood and Poole, and brakes and leg-rests are both desirable. The roads are chiefly chalk-flint, gravel, and limestone. Limestone N.W. of a line drawn through Westbury, Calne and Swindon. Chalk-flint south of this, to a line through Blandford, Fordingbridge and Winchester. Southward of this again, gravel.

WIMBORNE to SWANAGE (24 miles), *via* Wareham and Corfe Castle, Wimborne to Wareham, a distance of 13 miles, the surface is fair, but sandy here and there. Wareham to Corfe is 5 miles, all up-hill, not steep, but a soft surface; thence to Swanage it improves greatly.

ROMSEY to LYMINGTON (17 miles) *via* Cadman Bridge and Lyndhurst. The road is nearly all gravel. About 1¾ miles out of Romsey it is very steep, but after that there are only gentle undulations, and a good surface all the way.

ANDOVER to HINDON (30 miles), *via* Amesbury and Wiley. The roads have a flint surface all the way, and are very hilly. After the first three miles to Weyhill there are five or six hills, of about one mile each.

IRELAND.

Towards the West. Route I.

The following tour was performed in the Summer of 1872, by a Gentleman, riding a by no means powerful machine. Leaving Dublin in the morning, he went by Finglass to Ashford, about eight miles. From Ashford, the road work to Slane is through a charming country, the last three miles into Slane being down a decline, and affording capital rest to the rider. From Slane, where the *Boyne is crossed, the road rises almost imperceptibly to Dundrum, a small village with a 'Shebeen,' and beyond it, Carrickmacross. At the latter town there is an Inn where the traveller rested for the night, having traversed nearly 60 miles with ease. Starting again next day, he went viâ Castleblayney, a place full of historical interest— and Monaghan to Clogher, in Tyrone. From Clogher, the ride to Enniskillen is 20 miles, over good roads, and once arrived there, the tourist will find abundance of charming scenery in every direction To the north-west lies *Bundoran and the County Donegal; to the west is the County Sligo, and Lough Gill; while a day's journey in a south-westerly direction will bring the tourist to the famous **Connemara, where the almost unrivalled scenery is only equalled by the excellence of the roads.

The East. Route II.

In the east of Ireland, Wicklow is the county that attracts the tourist, and the rider of the bicycle will find here the value of his iron steed.   Twelve miles from Dublin there is Bray to be visited, and near it the famous **Dargle, as well as Lord Powerscourt's demesne with its *waterfall.   Beyond this, the tourist can visit the *"Glen of the Downs," The town of Wicklow, *"The Devil's Glen," *"Avoca," *" The Seven Churches," and many other scenes of beauty and interest, all of which are within easy reach of the bicyclist.

The South.   Route III.

In the extreme south west, the tour of Kerry will be found charming, but difficult.   Leaving Cork, whence *Blarney Castle may be reached by a fairly good road up the valley of the Lee (out and back in a short afternoon), by rail to Macroom the tourist proceeds viâ *Inchigeela and *Gougane Barra, to ***Glengariffe, to our mind the loveliest place in the three kingdoms.   There is fair bicycling ground in Lord Bantry's beautiful Park, admission to which is always obtainable.   Leaving Glengariffe, a steady ascent of about five miles, mostly too stiff for riding, brings the tourist to the tunnel under the crest of the Caha Mountains, which command one of the most *glorious views in the world.   This tunnel connects the counties of Cork and Kerry.   On the Kerry side there is a seven or eight mile descent, not too steep for a good rider, to the town of *Kenmare (where see R. C. Church and Convent, with its lace and its numerous publications), and then begin the ascent to the *Gap of Dunloe, about six miles, half of which must be walked. Time the journey so as to reach the Pass two hours before sunset, which will be easily done by leaving Glengariffe about 8 a.m. in summer time, or half-an-hour earlier in the autumn, thus leaving time for afternoon dinner at Kenmare.   The ride down to ***Killarney is marvellously beautiful, a couple of miles being on the level, past some mountain lakes that swarm with trout.   All about Killarney town and Mucross the roads are level and good.   From Killarney, a trip to Valentia Island will repay those riders who have plenty of time on their hands— or the route may be varied by taking the bold *coast road from Kenmare to Valentia, perfectly practicable, and thence proceeding to Killarney ; but on this journey the most commanding view of the Killarney **Lakes is lost, though the coast road has charms that nearly make up for it.   From Killarney, it will be better to return by rail, as the roads inland are neither good nor interesting.

The North.   Route IV.

In extent as well as in variety, this route is that which will best repay the bicycle tourist in Ireland.   He should take the train from Dublin to Newry, a dull town in a beautiful situation.   Hence proceed (roads good) to *Warren Point, 3½ miles ;   *Rosstrevor, 2½ ; *Kilkeel, 9½ ; Annalong, 5½ ; and *Newcastle, just over 7 ; the bold granite mountains of Mourne being all the time on the left, and *Carlingford Lough or the Irish Sea, on the right.   From Newcastle to Dundrum, 3½ miles, and Downpatrick, 10½ ; the roads are not so good nor so interesting. At Downpatrick, see Cathedral, and St. Patrick's grave.   From Downpatrick to Ballynahnch, 9½ ; and to Lisburn, 9½ ; and *Belfast, 8½ ; roads fair, and latterly very good.

The attractions of Belfast and its vicinity are best set forth in a Guide published for the Belfast Naturalists' Field Club, by Marcus Ward & Co., but as this may not be purchasable, the hotel keepers may be asked to borrow it for the tourist for a day.

Continuing the tour—the road to Carrickfergus, 9 miles, presents no difficulty; see *Castle ; thence to Larne, 9½ miles, it runs high, but not by any means impracticable—see *the Gobbins Cliffs, on Island Magee, the first of the northern basaltic rocks. Road to Glenarm, 11¼ miles, exquisite views, the road running pretty level along the top of chalk cliffs—*Glenarm Castle. Then to *Carnlough, 2½ miles; *Garron Point and *Cushendall, 10½ miles; the series of views are wonderful in their beauty, and the roads are proverbial through Ulster for their goodness. To *Cushendun, 4½ miles; and Ballycastle, 13½, (see *Grey Man's Path—a column of basalt, hanging across a gorge), the roads continue good, and the scenery becomes even bolder, the tourist being now fairly in the region of Columnar basalt, as at *Fairhead. To Ballintoy is 5½ miles; and close to the latter village is the wonderful swinging rope bridge of **Carrick-a-Rede. Hence to Bushmills, 7½ miles; one mile short of the town being the turning to the ***Giant's Causeway, for which see local guide books, as this whole work would fail to tell one tithe of its wonders. Bushmills to *Portrush, 7½ miles, admirable road, over basaltic and chalk cliffs. Portrush, fine watering place, to *Coleraine, beautifully situated town, road good, 5½ miles; or via *Portstewart 6½ miles. Coleraine to Garvagh, on the road lying west of the River Bann, 10½ miles, see *" Cutts," a waterfall, 16 feet high, whole width of the River Bann; to Magherafelt, 4½ miles; to Maghera, 5; to Castle Dawson, 5; roads as far as Maghera very good. To Toome (for *Lough-Neagh), 4 miles; to Randalstown, 5 miles; to Antrim, 4 miles; roads fair—Antrim *Round Tower, *Shane's Castle, Lord *Massareene's Gardens. By Muckamore to Belfast, 14¼ miles, over a range of hills. Splendid view of Belfast and its busy Lough, from the top of *Cave hill. See page 24 *ante* for the ride of "A.B.C." through Wales and Ireland.

HOTELS.

Dublin—*Shelburne*, *Jury's, Imperial*. Bray—*Marine*. Monkstown—*Murphy's*. Cork—*Imperial*. Glengariffe—*Eccles's*. Kenmare—*Lansdowne Arms.*—Killarney—*Mucruss Arms, *Railway, *Victoria, *Lake*. Valentia—*Fitzgerald Arms*. Lough Currane—*L.C. Hotel*. Newry—*Victoria*. Warrenpoint—*Victoria, Crown*. Lisburn—*Hertford Arms*. Belfast—*Imperial, *Royal, Commercial, Queen's*. Carrickfergus—*Victoria*. Larne—*King's Arms*. Glenarm—*Antrim Arms* Ballycastle—*Antrim Arms*. Giant's Causeway—*Coleman's*. Bushmills—*Doherty's, Reid's*. Portrush—*Antrim Arms, Coleman's*. Coleraine, —*Clothworker's Arms, Corporation Arms*. Antrim—*Massareene Arms*.

SCOTLAND.

ABERDEEN TO BLAIR ATHOLE.

Aberdeen to Park, 15 miles; Aboyne, 32 miles; Ballater, 36; Balmoral, 42; Braemar, 54; Blair Athole, 71.

NOTES ON THE ROAD.

This route can only be undertaken by the most sturdy, portions of the road being very bad, though not so throughout. All difficulties will be amply repaid by the glorious scenery through which you pass.

OBJECTS OF INTEREST.

Aberdeen is the third city of importance in Scotland, and of great antiquity, dating from the year 893. The motto of the Town Arms—*Bon-accord*—derives its origin from the fact of its being the watchword of the inhabitants when they expelled the English. Tourists in search of capital salmon-fishing cannot have better quarters or sport. Byron lived in his youth at 68, High Street, and the house is still named after him. Macbeth's death occured close to Culter. The site of the Roman Devana is also on this road, Especially noticeable on this trip are Drum House, Crathie Castle, and the Marquis of Huntley's seat, Aboyne Castle, all well calculated to repay the Bicyclist for the exertion necessary to cover indifferent roads.   Ballater is a fashionable spa, and likely to continue so till the rail is extended beyond this point. Few trips, of so short a distance, afford so much historical (ancient and modern) interest as this, in Scotland.   Balmoral, the favorite residence of the Queen, can be seen well in passing.   Tickets to view the Castle can only be obtained during her Majesty's absence,—or in other words, are not obtained during the season generally utilised by tourists, as her Majesty is seldom absent at this period of the year.   Braemar to Blair Athole yields a favourite pedestrian tour, and on this account alone will commend itself to bicyclists.   Ballatrich, close by, is the scene of Byron's early life.

HOTELS.

Aberdeen—*Douglas, Queen's, Imperial, Forsyth's*.   Blair Athole—*Athol Arms*.

BLAIR   ATHOLE   TO   PERTH.

Blair Athole to Kilicrankie, 3 miles ; Pitlochrie, 7 ; Dunkeld, 20 ; Stanley Junction, 24 ; Luncarty, 28 ; Perth, 32.

NOTES   ON   THE   ROAD.

This route presents few difficulties, the road being on the whole good.

OBJECTS   OF   INTEREST.

Blair Athole Castle is celebrated for its many historical associations. Kilicrankie Pass, celebrated for the battle, where Claverhouse, Viscount Dundee, fell. Glen Tilt, through which you pass, abounds with a whole series of magnificent cascades.   The enormous number of deer abounding on the Athole estates in perfect freedom, lends considerable interest to this route.   Perth, the " fair city " of Scotland, said to be the smallest, because it lies between two *Inches*.   Abernethy (of biscuit fame) is only 8½ miles from Perth, and should be visited on account of the fine specimens of round towers to be seen there.

HOTELS.

Perth—*Royal George, Pople's British, Queen's*.

GLASGOW   TO   DUMBARTON.

Glasgow to Dumbarton, 16 miles.

NOTES   ON   THE   ROAD.

The bicyclist will here be able to attain good speed, and alter his opinion of Scotch roads in general.

OBJECTS   OF   INTEREST.

Dumbarton was originally called Dun-Breton (Fort of the Britons).   It was here " the fause" Monteith betrayed Wallace.   His sword, measuring 5 feet 6 inches, may be seen in the Armory.

DUMFRIES   TO   GLASGOW.

Dumfries (1) to Holywood (2), 4 miles ; Closeburn (3), 12 miles ; Thorn Hill (4), 15 miles ; Sanguhar (5), 27 miles ; Kirkconnel (6), 30 miles ; New Cummock (7), 38 miles ; Mauchline (8), 50 miles ; Kilmarnock (9), 59 miles ; Glasgow (10), 72 miles.

(1)   St. Michael's Churchyard, see Burns' grave.

(2)   Grove of Sacred Druid Oaks, by the Parish Church.

(3)   Closeburn, the former seat of the Kirkpatricks'.

(4)   Thornhill, said to be cleanest village in Scotland, and outside, the Duke of Buccleuch's residence.

(5)   Intimately connected with the History of the Covenant.

(6)   Signifies " Parish of 50 Streams."

(7)   The Inventor of Gas, Wm. Murdock, born here.

(8)   Burns was married one mile from here.

(9)   Kilmarnock, Sir Wm. Wallace was educated at Riccarton, close by.

(10)   Glasgow, see the Necropolis.

NOTES ON THE ROAD.

From Kirkconnel to close on New Cummock, the road becomes more and more hilly.

HOTELS.

Dumfries—*King's Arms, Commercial and Railway.*   Kilmarnock—*The George, the Black, the Turf.*   Lanark—*Clydesdale, Black Bull.*   Glasgow—*Queen's, Carrick's, Royal George, Crown, Clarence.*

GLASGOW TO LANARK.

Glasgow to Motherwell, 9½ miles ; Motherwell to Carstairs, 18 miles ; Lanark, 23 miles.

NOTES ON THE ROAD.

For nearly the whole of this distance the roads are very good indeed, and there is nothing to daunt the most timid bicyclist.

OBJECTS OF INTEREST.

Lanark is celebrated as the town where the first Scottish Parliament assembled in 978. Wallace slew Haselrigg here, a sheriff of England, for the cowardly murder of his wife. There are several falls well worthy a visit in the immediate neighbourhood, viz., those of Bonnington (2½ miles distant), Corra Linn (3½ miles), Stonebyres, the largest fall, (6½ miles distant). The approach to this latter fall is by no means easy.

HOTELS.—Lanark—*Clydesdale, Commercial, Black Bull.*

CONCLUDING REMARKS.

It is very obvious that our British Tourists' Guide is neither exhaustive nor complete ; not exhaustive, because mere guide-book writing would fill many more pages than we can give in our book ; not complete, because bicycle riders have not as yet recorded their experiences of all the routes we have indicated. Our great aim has been *never to mislead a tourist,* and we have throughout, given only routes easily divisible into journeys traversable in an ordinary day. Unless this book were expanded to the size of the Post Office Directory, or to even more elephantine dimensions, it is manifestly impossible that it could usurp the functions of an English Baedeker or a Murray, nor is *that* our object. Messrs. Stanford, Wylde, Black, and others can be safely resorted to for sound, detailed information about British roads, British scenery, and British antiquities.

CHAPTER VII.

SWITZERLAND.

The Helvetian Republic would not at first sight appear to be attractive to bicycle riders, for the bicycle does not love mountains, and mountains are, in two senses, the most prominent features of Switzerland. Still in the western and northern cantons there are many trips that can be recommended. The majority of the guide books take Basle as their starting point, and for convenience sake, also because a Swiss Tour is a natural complement of the Tour of the Battlefields of 1870—we do the same.

Route I.

BASLE TO ZURICH—55 miles.

This road is perfectly practicable.

BASLE to BRUGG, 35 miles; BRUGG to ZURICH, 20 miles.

OBJECTS OF INTEREST.

Basle **Museum, with its picture gallery containing Rembrandts, Holbeins, Durers, Teniers, Caraccis.—On road, Rheinfels. Beyond Brugg, junction of *Three Rivers, and ancient Roman Settlement; * Königsfelden Abbey; *Hapsburgh Castle, the cradle of the House of Austria; Baden, *Ancient Castle, fine views; good views at intervals all the way.

HOTELS AT BASLE innumerable, and mostly good; try *Schreider, or *De la Cigogne. HOTELS AT ZURICH, *Bauer, *Bellevue.

Route II

ZURICH TO LUCERNE—38 miles.

Roads all round Lake of Zurich practicable. Views beautiful. First four miles towards Lucerne, easy, next four difficult. From Ober-Albis, gentle descent nearly all the way. At the fork beyond Ober-Albis take the road to the right, by Knonau and Wolfgang.

OBJECTS OF INTEREST.

At Zurich, see Great Minster, 11th-13th centuries; *Polytechnic School; Katz Castle; Arsenal. At Ober-Albis, ** view almost unequalled, including Pilatus, Rigi, Lakes of Zurich, Zug, Lucerne, and the Alps from the Sentis to the

Jungfrau. Round Lucerne few of the roads are practicable, that towards the Rigi is the best. Here see the Cathedral; the *Lion of Lucerne; Stauffer's Museum; the Arsenal; and the Town Hall, with its carvings and frescoes.

HOTELS AT LUCERNE, *Schweizerhof; *Swan.

Route III..

BASLE TO GENEVA—166 miles.

Roads practicable, with few exceptions, and these chiefly through the Münster Thal.

BASLE to BIENNE, 59 miles; BIENNE to NEUCHATEL, 18½ miles; NEUCHATEL to YVERDUN, 23 miles; YVERDUN to LAUSANNE, 26½ miles; LAUSANNE to GENEVA, 39 miles.

OBJECTS OF INTEREST.

On the road from Basle (see Route I), several battlefields. Grand Pass called *Münster Thal, a Roman road; at Pertius, the watershed north and south; at *Sonceboz, a fine view of the Alps, from Mont Blanc to the Jungfrau. At Bienne, good hotel, and an excursion may be made here to Soleure. Road hence to Neuchatel by the side of the Lake of Bienne. From Yverdun (*Castle) to Lausanne and Ouchy, by the side of the Lake all the way, gives fine views of the Alps. At Chavornay, the road is somewhat difficult; at *Champmont is a fine old Castle; at Lausanne, see Cathedral; *Gibbon's House, with its fine view of the Alps; and go on to Ouchy on the Lake of Geneva. From Ouchy, a branch route to Vevey is practicable. To Geneva by Morges, Nyon, and Coppet, marvellous views of the Alps all the way.

HOTELS.

MUNSTER, "Krone." SONCEBOZ, * "Krone." BIENNE, * "De Jura." NEUCHATEL, * "Du Lac." YVERDUN, "De Londres." LAUSANNE, "Faucon," * "Gibbon." OUCHY, ** "Beau Rivage." GENEVA, innumerable—any on the Lake good, but try * "Hotel Beau Rivage and Métropole.

Route IV.

GENEVA TO BERNE—89 miles.

Lausanne, 39 miles; Freiburg, 30; Berne, 20; roads fair.

OBJECTS OF INTEREST.

At Geneva, see various views of the Savoy Alps; Mont Blanc Bridge; * Relief of Mont Blanc; * Russian Church; * Public Library; * Cathedral; * Musée Rath.

From LAUSANNE to FREIBURG,* fine views on the right of the road. At Romont, fine old Castle; at Freiburg a wonderful suspension * bridge, 905 feet long, 180 high, 23 wide, nearly twice the length of the Menai bridge; cost £24,000 sterling. Another suspension *bridge, 640 feet long and 317 feet high. *Cathedral, A.D. 1300. On road Freiburg to Berne, fine view of Oberland.

HOTELS.

FREIBURG, *Zähringer Hof," "Kramern." BERNE, "Bernerhof," *"Bellevue," * "De France."

Route V.

BERNE TO INTERLAKEN—36 miles.

In Berne, visit *Minster ; Bear Pit ; *Terrace, with view of Berner Alps ; Museum ; old houses in main streets ; fountains ; Federal Council Hall ; *Roman Catholic Church.

Good road to Thun, 18 miles. Thence along south side of Lake, 15 miles, fair going ; through Unterseen, 3 miles ; Interlaken Valley, capital bicycling ground.

OBJECTS OF INTEREST.

Mountains on right of road to Thun, the Stockhorn and the Neisen. At Thun, its picturesque situation ; Military College ; * Castle of Schadau ; fine views all the way along to Interlaken, there excursions may be undertaken to Lauterbrunnen and Grindelwald, but the road up is impracticable for more than three miles, but both forks are practicable down.

HOTELS.

THUN, *Bellevue," " Kreuz." INTERLAKEN, innumerable, try *"Oberlanderhof," *"Victoria," *"Jungfraublick." ZWEILUTSCHINEN, " Bâr." LAUTERBRUNNEN, *"Capricorn." GRINDELWALD, *" Bâr." " Adler," " Eiger," " Glacier."

THE BATTLEFIELDS OF 1870.

This interesting and practicable trip may be made a link between the Belgian and the Swiss tours. Breaking off the Belgian trip at Liege or Spa, the bicyclist will do well to proceed by rail *via* Namur to Mezieres.

Starting thence, he will in 13 miles reach ***Sedan, and in two more **Bazeilles, the roads being fairly good. A whole day may be well spent here on the terrible battlefield of September 1st, 1870. Road to Carignan, 5¾ miles fair ; but preferably take Southern Route Nationale to *Stenay, 16 miles; then to Montmedy 6 miles ; then S.E. to Longuyon, 15 miles, and S. to *Etain, 16 miles, This was the route operated on by the armies of MacMahon and the Crown Prince before the Catastrophe of Sedan. From Etain 17 miles leads (moderate road E.) to ***Gravelotte, where *Vionville, *Rezonville, and other battles of the 16th and 18th August, were fought between the armies of the Red Prince and Bazaine. Near Vionville, cross the new German frontier. and reach ***Metz in 7 miles. Total—to Metz from Mezieres, 92 miles, English.

From Metz, Route Nationale E. to St. Avold, 21 miles; thence to **Forbach and **Saarbruck, 16 miles, this last road being not so good. National Road hence to Sarreguimines, 9 miles ; *Bitsche, poor road, 18 miles ; *Neiderbronn, on National road, 9 miles ; **Woerth, or Reichshoffen, 4 miles ; *Hagenau, 5 miles ; ***Strasbourg, 16 miles. Total—Metz to Strasbourg, 98 miles : all this line of country comprising the scenes of the first fighting in 1870, except the Field of *Wissembourg, which can be reached by branch trip of 15 miles, good road, or rai from Hagenau.

HOTELS.

MEZIERES, " Palais Royal," " Postes."　SEDAN, " *Croix d'Or," "De l'Europe."
MONTMEDY (small house) ; ETAIN (do.).　METZ, *" De Metz," *" Imperiale,"
" D' l'Europe."　SAARBRUCK, two (good, small).　NIEDERBRONN, three (good,
small).　HAGENAU, two (good, small).　STRASBOURG (all good).　*Maison Rouge,
" De Paris," "d'Angleterre," " De France."

OBJECTS OF INTEREST, beside Battlefields, include, at Sedan—the Weaver's
Cottage, where Bismarck met Napoleon ; Chateau de Bellevue, where Napoleon
surrendered to the German Emperor ; Graves at Gravelotte ; Fortification and
Barracks at Metz, also *Cathedral (called " the Lantern of France," as Bath
Abbey is " the Lantern of England;") Mineral Springs at Neiderbronn, and
Cemetery commanding view of Wöerth field ; Hagenau, Church and dismantled
Fortifications ; Strasbourg, *Cathedral, Fortifications—especially the Porte des
Pierres, near which was the breach ; the two Cemeteries, and the German
extension Field-works.

UPPER RHINE.

There is little to interest the tourist on the western side of the Rhine from
Strasbourg to Basle, but two good roads will be a paradise for bicyclists.　The
upper road runs through the towns of Schelestadt, a fortress ; Colmar, and
Mühlhausen, great factory places ; from Cernay, a short trip of 18 miles to the
fortress of Belfort, on French territory, being practicable.　On the lower and
shorter road, which is also made level, there is only one stopping place—New
Breisach, about midway, and the road is as level as the river Rhine.

DISTANCES.—Lower Road : Strasbourg to New Breisach, 40 miles ; New
Breisach to Basle, 35 miles.　Upper Road : Strasbourg to Colmar, 36 miles ;
Colmar to Cernay, 24 miles ; Cernay to Basle, 23 miles.

HOTELS.

COLMAR, " à la Gare."　MUHLHAUSEN, " Elsass."　BELFORT, "L'Ancienne
Poste."　NEW BREISACH (small house at the ferry).

BELGIUM.

Route I.

ANTWERP to MALINES, 14 miles ; MALINES to BRUSSELS, 18 miles.　Roads
like tables.　At Antwerp see *Cathedral (Rubens' pictures, carved pulpit and
iron west gate) ; St. Jacques (Rubens' altar piece, and Vandyke's pictures) ;
*Museum (pictures by Matsys, Rubens, Vandyke).　At Malines, see *Cathedral,
and St. Rumbold's, Notre Dame, and St. John's (all three latter Rubens' pictures).
On road to Brussels, pass Royal Palace, at Laeken.　At Brussels, Boulevards
mostly afford fine riding ground.　See *Cathedral, *Hotel de Ville, *Museum
(pictures by Caracci, Guido, Veronese, Velasquez, Cuyp, Teniers, Perugino,
Rubens), Lace-shops, *Park, *Bois de la Cambre, Church of Notre Dame de la
Chapelle, Church of the Sablon, *Porte de Hal, Gallery St. Hubert, Zoological
Gardens.

BRUSSELS.—HOTELS innumerable—try "l'Europe," "De Saxe," "De Flandre," * "Horton's." ANTWERP HOTELS—*" St. Antoine," " de l'Europe," " Grand Laboreur," " De la Paix."

Route II.

OSTEND TO BRUSSELS.

Ostend to Bruges, 16 miles. Road very flat. At Bruges, see *Cathedral, Church of Notre Dame (pictures and carvings), *Hospital of St. John, *Town Hall and Chapel of St Sang, *Belfry, *Lace-working, *Fish Market, Museum (pictures by Van Eyck). Take the canal path, if permitted, to Ghent, 33 miles but the road by Nevale is good.

At Ghent, see Cathedral interior, lined with black marble, and paintings by the Van Eycks and Rubens, also wood carvings; Beguinage Convent, City Library (valuable MS.), Museum and Academy; quaint old Spanish houses.

Ghent to Brussels, splendid road by Denderleeu and Assche, 33 miles. For Brussels, see Route I, Belgium.

HOTELS.

OSTEND, "Ship," " Fontaine," " Royal de Prusse," " Mertian's."
At BRUGES, Schupp's " Hotel de Flandre," " De Commerce," " De Londres."
At GHENT, " De la Poste," " Royal," " De Vienne."

Route III.

BRUSSELS TO LIÉGE.

Take the south road to Waterloo, 13 miles ; thence across the famous field by Mont St. Jean and La Belle Alliance to Quatre Bras, 9 miles. At these cross roads, take the one to the east to Namur, 18 miles. Here see Church of St. Loup, interior porphyry and black marble. From thence to Liége the road runs parallel with the railway on opposite sides of the Meuse, to Huy, 22 miles ; then on same side to Liége, 19 miles, the gradients being difficult near the end of this journey.

At Liége, see *Cathedral, and all the other Churches are worth visiting; the Palace, *the large Iron Works.

HOTELS.

NAMUR, " Bellevue," " D'Harscamp." LIéGE, " D'Angleterre," " De Suede," " De France."

Route IV.

LIÉGE TO SPA.

By Louyegne (half-way), 25 miles ; Road sinuous and hilly, scenery very fine, and good grounds around Spa for bicycling in the public walks.

HOTELS.

SPA.—" D'York," " Des Pays Bas," " Bellevue."

Route V.

LIÉGE TO COLOGNE.

Road poor, but wonderfully beautiful and somewhat shorter than railway; about 17 miles to Verviers, by Chenée and Chaudefontaine, 5 miles from Liege, and a lovely place. At Verviers, see important factories. At Herbesthal, 5 miles, across frontier to Germany. To Aix la Chapelle, road practicable, 9 miles. At Aix or Aachen, see * Cathedral (burial place of Charlemagne), and new Church; *Public Gardens and Fountains; *Aerolite weighing three tons. Aix to Juliers, 20 miles, road good; Juliers viâ Bergheim, road also good, to Cologne 27 miles. The road by Duren is a little shorter but not so good.

HOTELS.

Chaudefontaine, " Des Bains." Verviers, "Du Chemin de Fer." Cologne, *" Disch," *" Bellevue," " Victoria," *" Du Nord."

OBJECTS OF INTEREST.

At Cologne, see **Cathedral and Treasury of the Three Kings; Churches of *St. Martin, St. Maria in Capitolio, St. Cunibert, the Apostles, St. Peter's, St. Ursula's; the *Museum, its Stained Glass and Roman Antiquities; the Zoological Gardens; and near Cologne, the Dechen Grotto. Also ask for the old *Roman Amphitheatre.

GERMANY.

It is just possible for a bicyclist to do the Rhine from Cologne to Coblenz, by the road which runs at an average of $1\frac{1}{2}$ miles from the banks behind the town of Bonn; but there is nothing to repay him for his trouble, and if he wants to see the Rhine, he had better go by the boat to Bingen, in the ordinary way.

HOLLAND

Has, naturally, fine level roads, but they are far from interesting, though they are in general well shaded by trees, and are consequently agreeable in summer time. The only routes we can recommend as of general interest, are

ROTTERDAM TO THE HAGUE.

This is only fourteen miles in length, and is throughout entirely level riding. Before leaving Rotterdam, see the *Boompjes walk, the Cathedral and its Organ, Erasmus's House in the Kerk-Straat. At the Hague, the seat of Government, see *Museum (Dutch masters), the Old Palace, the New Palace, Zoological Gardens, the Palace in the Wood, and four miles from the New Palace, the fine watering-place of Scheveningen, the road to which is perfect for bicycle exercise, and is planted with old elms and oaks, forming a beautiful avenue.

THE HAGUE TO AMSTERDAM

Is also a level road about 21 miles long, and well shaded in parts. At the capital of Holland, see the *Two Great Ship Canals, the *Hooge Sluis Bridge and its view, the *Palace, built on piles like the rest of the city; the Oude-Mannen Huis and its paintings; *Rijk's Museum, fine collection of Dutch masters; the Crystal Palace; Zoological Gardens, the Oude Kerk and the Nieuwe Kerk; the Royal and other Docks; * Coster's, for diamond cutting; five miles off, the show-village of Broek is worth seeing, and at Zaandam is Peter the Great's House carefully preserved.

———

HOTELS.

ROTTERDAM, " Victoria," " New Bath," *" Pays Bas," " Stads Herberg."
HAGUE, " Bellevue," " Vieux Doelen," " Paulez."
AMSTERDAM, *" Old Bible."   AMSTOL, " Doelen."

From these centres short bicycle trips may be extemporised in every direction, with the greatest facility.

FRANCE.

———

The following important decree relating to Bicycles has been made public in Paris :—

"November 17th, 1874.

"Seeing that complaints are often addressed to us on the subject of accidents caused by velocipedes, which run to and fro without control; seeing, however, that they are not only an amusement, but, to some people, are of great utility; that to forbid the circulation of bicycles on the public road would prejudice interests worthy attention," &c , &c., "it is ordered that velocipedes. in the day-time, shall carry bells loud enough to be heard at a distance; must be lighted at night-fall with a lamp or lanterns, like those of cabs; must be numbered, if to let, and bear the name and address of their owner. Persons not attending to these rules, will have their bicycles forfeited, and will be prosecuted."

FRENCH TARIFF ON BICYCLES.

"Velocipedes, in the Conventional tariff, come under the category of ' carriages,' and are therefore liable to a duty of 10 per cent. on their value."

There is so little of interest in Picardy, in comparison with other almost as accessible provinces of France, that we do not care to waste our space in dealing with a route from Calais to Paris. We therefore commence with

DIEPPE AND HAVRE TO PARIS.

Route I.

Newhaven to Dieppe, or Southampton to Havre. We strongly recommend the rail as far as Rouen, or the coast road by Fecamp to Havre, 65 miles, or one day's nice work.

From Havre the road follows the valley of the Seine all the way. *Harfleur ancient Port of Normandy, 4½ miles; Beuzeville, 12 miles; Nintot, 4 miles; *Yvetot, 7 miles, famous for Beranger's Roi d'Yvetot, parent of Thackeray's King of Brentford; Motteville, 5 miles; Pavilly, 7 miles; Malaunay, 6½ m. (viaduct); Rouen, 6 miles.

ROUEN TO PARIS.

Oissel, 10 miles; *Pont de l'Arche, 3¼ miles, fine bridge, fine church; St. Pierre de Vouvray, 8 miles; Gaillon, 9½ miles, *the first vineyards;* *Vernon, 9 miles, fine church and bridge; Bonnières, 7 miles; Rosny, 4½ miles; Mantes, 4 miles, one of the prettiest towns in France, occupying the midst of the best part of the Seine valley. Here see Cathedral, so called, and fine bridge. Epone, 5 miles; Triel, 8 miles, end of the lofty limestone cliffs, and commencement of quieter but equally lovely scenery; St. Germain, 10 miles, beautiful road, Royal Palace, Tomb of James II. of England; enter Paris by the Rond Point de Courbevoie and the Champs Elysées.

OBJECTS OF INTEREST.

DIEPPE Churches, *St. Jacques, St. Rémi; the Chateau, fine view; the Plage and the Baths; the fishing suburb of Le Pollet. and four miles off, good road, the famous **Chateau D'Arques, where the League were finally defeated by Henry IV.

HAVRE, the Docks, the Fortifications; Ingouville Church.

FECAMP, *Notre Dame Abbey, where the liqueur "Benedictine" is made.

ROUEN Cathedral, Churches of **St. Ouen, St. Maclou, *St. Patrice (fine glass); the Palace, *Place de la Pucelle, Hotel de Ville, Hotel de la Préfecture, Clock Tower, Palais de Justice, Cotton and Sugar Factories.

HOTELS.

DIEPPE, " Royal," " De la Plage," " Des Bains."

ROUEN, Smith's *" Albion," " D'Angleterre," " Normandie," "Victoria," (small.)

Route II.

THE LOIRE.

Steamer, Liverpool to Nantes, or (see Route III), S. Malo to Dinan, Ploermel, Redon, Savernay, Nantes. Nantes to Oudon, 10½ miles, fine old Castle; Ancencis, 6 miles, old Chateau; Ingrandes, 13 miles; La Poissonière 13 miles, splendid Chateau and Park; Angers, 12 miles, *Cathedral, Chateau, *St. Serge's, Hotel Dieu, Gallery of Copies of all David's Pictures.

Angers to St. Mathurin, 14¼ miles; Les Rosieries, 9½ miles; Langeois, 17 miles; Tours, 16½ miles, scenery very fine, road fair, mostly along the river side; castles and vineyards on every hand.

Tours, see *Cathedral, fine view from north tower; Chateau, Palais de Justice, Bridge, Chateau of Plessis les Tours, the Prefecture. Fine streets and good exercise ground between the Loire and the Cher. Hence to Nevers either along the valley of the Cher, roads poor, by Vierzon, Bourges (great Arsenal and head-quarters of the Army of the Loire, in the Autumn of 1870) ; or preferably by the Loire valley, thus:

Tours to Blois, roads fair ; *Amboise, 15 miles; splendid old Castle, built by Julius Cæsar ; Blois, 20 miles. Here note Castle, Cathedral, Allées promenade, fine view from the Bridge. Blois to Orleans : Menars, 5½ (five miles from this is the *Chateau de Chambord (containing 440 rooms), in a fine forest with wild boars) ; Beaugency, 14½, fine Castle, scene of a thousand battles, ancient and modern, from A.D. 450 to 1871 ; Meung, 4½, old Castle ; Orleans, 12. At Orleans, note *Cathedral, St. Pierre's and St. Aignan's, Hotel de Ville, Museum, fine old Gothic houses ; also effects of capture and re-capture during the late war.

A continuation of this route may be made to Nevers, and through Western Burgundy to Lyons.

HOTELS.

NANTES, " De France," " Du Commerce."   ANGERS, " Cheval Blanc," " Le Roy."   TOURS, *" Bordeaux," *" De l'Univers."   AMBOISE, " Lion d'Or." BLOIS, " D'Angleterre."   ORLEANS, " D'Orleans, " Boule d'Or," " Du Loiret." NEVERS, " De France."

Route III.

ACROSS BRITTANY.

Steamer, Southampton to S. Malo.   At S. Malo, visit Fortifications, *Cathedral.   Cross the Harbour to Dinard, thence good road to Dinan, 21 miles. Dinan is a most picturesque town, beautifully situated on River Rance, the estuary of which above S. Malo should not be missed.   Old walls of Dinan and great Viaduct, well worth seeing.   Dinan to Caulnes, 30 miles, splendid ride through Forest and rich country ; two miles stiff ascent, then a ride of more than 20 miles either level, or a gentle descent.   Superb views over half Brittany. Caulnes to Ploermel, 28 miles, level road ; Ploermel famous for its " Pardon," or Saint's Festival, even in Saint-celebrating Brittany; fine old Church.   Redon, 30 miles, along the valley of the Artz.   At Redon, *old Clock Tower, fine Chateau ; then by Pont Chateau and Savernay, to Nantes, 34 miles.

HOTELS.

S. MALO, " *Chateaubriand."   DINAN, " De Commerce," " De la Poste." PLOERMEL, " De France," " De Commerce."   REDON, " Lion d'Or." NANTES (see Route II).

Route IV.

PARIS TO CHERBOURG.

To Rosny (reverse part of Route I). At Rosny, take southern road, *Pacy, 14 miles, fine Church; *Evreux, 10 miles (67 miles from Paris); *Cathedral, founded by Henry I. of England, St. Taurin's Church, Clock Tower, Bishop's Palace. Evreux to Marche Neuf, 25 miles, fair road; Lisieux, 20 miles, good road; *Cathedral (A.D. 1022), and expiatory Chapel for Jean d'Arc; fine old timbered houses, Bishop's Palace and *Gardens. *Moult, 21½ miles, and Mondeville, with its caves, from the stone of which Westminster Abbey was built; *Caen, 8 miles, the old Capital of Normandy. See all the Churches, Norman in style, especially S. Etienne's, burial place of William the Conqueror; Library of 48,000 vols.; Palais de Justice, Museum, Lace-making. Bayeux, 19 miles; see *Tapestry, wrought by Queen Matilda, wife of the Conqueror, representing his victory over England; *Cathedral, built by William's brother Odo, A.D. 1077; Hotel de Ville. Isigny, 22 miles, at the head of a pretty Bay; Carentan, 6 miles, fine Church, ruined Castle; Valognes, 30½ miles further, bad roads, Castle of William the Conqueror, fine College and Library; Cherbourg, 17 miles. Here see Hotel de Ville (picture gallery), *Dockyard and Arsenal (in which Napoleon "renewed the wonders of Egypt"); *the Breakwater, and its Forts. Steamers hence to Southampton.

HOTELS.

Evreux, " Du Grand Cerf." Lisieux, " De France."

Caen, " D'Angleterre," " Place Royale."

Bayeux, " Du Luxembourg," " Grand." Cherbourg, " l'Univers," " l'Aigle."

CHAPTER VIII.

On Clubs.

Rules for the Club, for the Road, for the Race.

In appending a list of Bicycle Clubs, with the names of the officers and the addresses of the various Head-Quarters, so far as it has been possible to ascertain them, we cannot but submit, as a suggestion to the bicycling world, the expediency of such a federation of clubs as would lead to the substitution of one set of rules for the number that at present exist. The Football Clubs have recently, very much to the common convenience, adopted a uniform set of rules ; and we feel assured that if the Bicycle Clubs were to appoint delegates to a central meeting in London, the expediency of such a step would be at once, and unanimously, admitted. We would advocate the formation of a Central Club in London, at which members of any country clubs, duly affiliated, would be made welcome, and be furnished with advice, and with practical help if necessary ; members of the London Clubs being of course similarly treated on their arrival in any provincial town in which a club may exist. The Editor of this work will be glad to receive adhesions to this movement, which seems more essential to Bicyclists than to any other kind of athletes.

METROPOLITAN BICYCLE CLUBS.

AMATEUR.—" Amateur B.C."—H. N. Custance, Esq., *Hon. Sec.* and *Capt.*

ARIEL.—" Ariel B C."—

THE LONDON, Clarendon Chambers, Charing Cross.—J. Inwards, Esq., *President ;* — Nevill, Esq., *Captain ;* A. W. Barrett, Esq., *Hon. Sec.*

MIDDLESEX.—" Middlesex B.C."—" King's Arms " Hotel, High Street, Kensington.—Chas. Spencer, Esq., *President ;* Amiè Boura, Esq., *Vice-President ;* H. C. Walker, Esq., *Captain ;* F. Tyne, Esq., *Hon. Sec.*

PICKWICK.—" Pickwick B.C." Mitford Tavern, Hackney. — Yeoman, Esq., *Captain ;* Lamartine C. B. Yeoman, Esq., *Hon. Sec.*

ST. GEORGE'S.—" St. George's B.C."—

SURREY.—" Surrey B. C."—T. F. Garrett, Esq., *President ;* James Copland, Esq., *Vice-President ;* R. T. Causton, Esq., *Captain ;* A. Howard, Esq., *Hon. Sec.* 5, Godliman Street, Doctor's Commons.

TENSION.—" Tension B.C."—Stoke Newington Green.

PROVINCIAL BICYCLE CLUBS.

BIRMINGHAM—"Aston Star Club" (established 1869), 52, Park Lane, Aston New Town. Oldest club in existence.—J. R. Whitehouse, Esq., *President;* F. Whitehouse, Esq., *Captain;* T. Williams, Esq., *Hon. Sec.*

BRIGHTON.—"Brighton Bicycle Club," 14, Queen's Road.—Charles Bucknell, Esq., *President;* Richard Peek, Esq., *Vice-President;* Robert Walls, Esq., *Captain;* R. Harrison, Esq., *Hon. Sec.*

CAMBRIDGE.—"Cambridge University Bicycle Club.—Hon. J. W. Plunkett (Trinity College), *President;* Hon. Ion Keith Falconer (Trinity College), *Vice-President;* A. E. James, Esq. *Hon. Sec.*

COVENTRY.—"The Coventry Bicycle Association."—J. Thomas, Esq., *President;* A. C. Hickling, Esq., *Vice-President;* A. Dennis, Esq., *Hon. Sec.;* A. Clarke, Esq., *Treasurer.*

MANSFIELD.—"The Mansfield Bicycle Club."—"Nag's Head," Westgate, Mansfield.—C. R. Hoare, Esq., *Hon. Sec.;* J. Edmonds, Esq., *Treasurer;* W. G. Jackson, Esq., *Captain;* F. Sargent, Esq., *Sub-Captain.*

NORTHAMPTON.—"True Briton B.C.," "True Briton," Maple Street. Northampton.—Charles Hutchins, Esq., *President;* Edward Gilbert, Esq., *Treasurer;* Alfred Pacey, Esq., *Secretary.*

"The Northampton Star Bicycle Club."—"Cross Keys" Hotel, Sheep Street.—Charles Smith, Esq., *Treasurer;* Charles Tyrrell, Esq. *Captain;* Walter Frisby, Esq., *Hon. Sec.*

OXFORD.—"The Dark Blue Bicycle Club—24, "New Inn," Hall Street, Oxford.—C. Penrose, Esq. (Oriel), *Captain;* A. B. Carpenter, Esq., New College, *Hon. Sec.*

PORTSMOUTH.—"Portsmouth Bicycle Club"—Museum Gardens, Kingston, Portsea.—J. E Buck, Esq., *Chairman.*

SHEFFIELD.—"Sheffield and Hallamshire B.C."— Club House, "Hallamshire Hotel,' West Street, Sheffield.— Thomas Harley, Esq., *President;* Walter Crisman, Esq., *Vice-President;* Henry Wilson, Esq., *Captain;* W. K. Hydes, Esq., *Treasurer;* Harry Turner, Esq., *Hon. Secretary.*

WOLVERHAMPTON.—"Sun B.C."—"Sun" Inn, Commercial Road. — Heaton, Esq., *Chairman;* — Wilcox, Esq., *Vice-Chairman;* J. B. Penn, Esq., *Hon. Sec.;* W. Turner, Esq., *Treasurer;* R. Evans, Esq., *Captain;* S. Perks, Esq., *Jun. Captain.*

CLUB RULES

For the guidance of such gentlemen as may be desirous of forming Bicycle Clubs, we subjoin three sets of Club rules, and also rules for the Road, and for Club racing, with form of Entry, which appear to us drawn up in a sense calculated to promote the enjoyment of Bicycling, in a social and systematic manner.

CAMBRIDGE UNIVERSITY.

I. That this Club be called the "CAMBRIDGE UNIVERSITY BICYCLE CLUB," and that it be open to members of the University of Cambridge only.

II. That the officers consist of President and Secretary, the latter to fill the office of Treasurer.

III. That a General Meeting of the Club be held at the end of each term, when the officers for the ensuing term shall be elected by ballot, the retiring officers being eligible for re-election.

IV. That the officers and two other members of the club shall constitute the committee, the two members to be elected at the last general meeting in each term.

V. The officials are empowered to call the first meeting in each term.

VI. The Committee shall be the governing body of the club; shall have power to call special meetings of the club for any purpose whatever; to expel any member upon due cause being shown; to suspend any officer; to appoint days for excursions; to manage and control the expenditure of the club; and do all such others acts and things as they may deem necessary for carrying out the objects of the club.

VII. That any candidate for admission to the club must send his name in to the Secretary, and shall be balloted for by the members of the committee at their next meeting; two black balls to exclude.

VIII. In case of a vacancy among the officers or members of the committee, the committee shall immediately appoint another member to the place of the office vacated; and the officer or member so appointed shall hold office until the next general meeting of the club, when either he or some other member shall be duly elected thereto.

IX. The President shall preside at all committee, general and special meetings, and a Vice-President shall be elected at the last general meeting in each term, who shall, in the absence of the President, represent him in all respects.

X. The President shall give at least one day's notice of his being unable to attend a meeting.

XI. All monies shall be received and paid by the Treasurer, and he shall keep an account thereof; but he shall not make any disbursement whatever without being first authorized by the committee, of which a resolution duly recorded in the minute-book shall be sufficient proof.

XII. The Treasurer shall, in retiring from office, present his accounts to the club.

XIII. The committee shall draw up a code of bye-laws for regulating the excursions of the club, and shall have the power of altering or adding to them as they may deem necessary.

XIV. Gentlemen who have been members of the club and are not in residence, shall be considered honorary members.

XV. The entrance fee shall be five shillings; and the subscription five shillings each term.

XVI. That these rules shall not be altered or added to except by the consent of a majority of the members of the club; and any amendment or addition thereunto must be voted upon at one of the general meetings only.

Bye-Laws.

(For the Regulation of Excursions.)

1. That due notice shall be given to each member of the club, of the time and place of meeting for each excursion; and that this notice be posted on the screens of each college.

2. That the President shall have entire control during all excursions; and (for the safety of the public) of compelling members to stop or dismount when passing horses, &c. Any member infringing this rule shall be liable to a fine of half-a-sovereign, and shall cease to be a member of the club until the fine be paid.

3. That members shall wear the uniform of the club (*i.e.* ribbon and jacket) at all club meets.

DARK BLUE (OXFORD).

1.—That this Club be called the "Dark Blue Bicycle Club."

2.—That the objects of the Club be the holding of meets and races, and the arrangement of tours.

3.—That the power of election be vested in the whole Club. Candidates must be proposed by a member of the Club. The Hon. Secretary shall give notice of the proposal, and if no ballot is demanded within seven days, the candidates shall be declared elected.

5.—That in the ballot one black ball in ten be sufficient to exclude.

6.—That the Officers of the Club be a Captain, and Hon. Secretary and Treasurer.

7.—That the election of Officers take place every year, the same officers being re-eligible.

8.—That there be a Committee, consisting of the Officers of the Club, with three other members, with power to add to their number. Three members shall constitute a quorum.

9.—That the business of the Club be transacted by the Committee, except as otherwise ordered by the Rules.

10.—That the Captain preside at all meetings, and exercise a general authority over the business of the Club.

11.—That the Hon. Secretary and Treasurer conduct the correspondence of the Club, receive the subscriptions, and keep the accounts.

12.—That each member provide himself with the distinguishing badge of the Club, to be carried on all occasions when riding.

13.—That the subscription be five shillings a term, payable in advance, with an entrance subscription of five shillings.

14.—That any member who shall be fourteen days in arrear with his subscription, be liable to be excluded from the Club, but may be readmitted on payment of entrance subscription.

1.—Any Competitor going a different route to the one laid down will be disqualified.

2.—Any Competitor using other means of locomotion to win the race than his bicycle or legs will be disqualified.

3.—Any Competitor riding on the footpath will be disqualified.

4.—Each Competitor will have a number on his left breast corresponding to his number on the Programme.

RULES TO BE OBSERVED BY PROFESSIONAL RIDERS.

These are the oft quoted Wolverhampton Rules.

1.—Riders must pass each other on the outside, and be a clear length of the bicycle in front before taking the inside; and the inside man must allow room for his competitor to pass.

2.—One attendant only shall be allowed in the dressing room, or on the course, with each rider, and he must not touch the machine at starting.

3.—If the judge is convinced that two riders arrange for the winner to divide any prize, they shall be disqualified, and the prize given for a race at the next meeting.

4.—If a rider fails to appear in time, his partner shall run with another. No walk over will be allowed.

5.—In order that the course may be in as good condition as possible for competitors, no practising will be allowed on the day of the race.

The number of each rider will be shown on the telegraph-board at starting, and the number of the winner of each heat.

RULES OF A PROVINCIAL CLUB.

1. The Club shall be called the " ——————— Bicycle Club," and the place of meeting shall be at ——————— ——————— ——————— or at such other place as the Committee shall decide.

2. The Officers of the Club shall consist of a Captain, Secretary, Treasurer, and two Auditors.

3. The Officers shall be elected at the general meetings of the Club to be held in the months of December and June, and shall be eligible for re-election.

4. The Officers and three other members of the Club shall constitute the Committee. The three members shall be elected at every general meeting. Retiring members shall always be eligible for re-election.

5. The annual general meeting shall be held during the month of December.

6. The Committee shall meet the first Wednesday night in every month at eight o'clock, for the purpose of transacting the business of the Club, and four shall form a quorum.

7. The Committee shall be the governing body of the Club; shall have power to call special meetings of the Club for any purpose whatever; to expel any member of the Club upon due cause being shown; to suspend any Officer; to appoint meeting days for exercise and excursions; to manage and control the expenditure of the Club; to fix and arrange for races, and the value and number of prizes to be contested for thereat; and to do all such other acts and things as they may deem necessary for the carrying out the objects of the Club.

8. In every case the decision of the Committee shall be final unless notice of appeal in writing be given to the Secretary by any member, whether aggrieved thereby or not, on or before the next Wednesday night following that on which the decision or resolution to be appealed against was arrived at or made.

9. All appeals from the Committee shall be to the Club, and shall be heard at the next special or general meeting, and the decision of such meeting shall in every instance be final.

10. In case of the suspension of any officer or a vacancy occurring in the officers or in the members of the Committee, the Committee shall immediately appoint another in the stead of the one suspended or vacating office, and the officer or member so appointed shall hold office until the next general meeting, when he or some other member shall be duly elected thereto.

11. Any Officer suspended by the Committee shall forthwith, upon written notice thereof to him, give up to the person appointed to receive the same, all Books, documents, monies, and effects belonging to the Club.

12. No alterations in or amendments to these Rules shall be made except at a general or special meeting of the Club.

13. The Captain shall preside at all Committee and general and special meetings. He shall immediately on election appoint a deputy, who shall act in his stead on all occasions in his absence.

14. The Secretary shall keep a list of members of the Club, with residence and occupation, and date of entry, and leaving or expulsion; a book containing minutes of all meetings; of persons present, and of all resolutions carried; and the business transacted thereat. The Secretary shall, if possible, attend all meetings, and, if absent, shall always appoint a deputy.

15. All monies shall be received and paid by the Treasurer, and he shall keep an account thereof, but he shall not make any disbursement whatever without being first authorized thereto by the Committee, of which a resolution duly recorded in the minute-book shall be sufficient proof.

16. The Treasurer shall report at every Committee meeting the amount of money in hand, and shall obtain the instructions of the Committee as to all necessary disbursements.

17. The Auditors shall inspect the accounts and the Books of the Club at the annual general meeting, and report thereon.

18. The Books of the Club kept by the various Officers thereof, shall be open at all reasonable times for inspection by any member.

19. The votes of the majority of members present and voting at any meeting (except as mentioned in the next rule) shall be decisive, and, where the votes are equal, the Chairman shall have a casting vote.

20. Any person desiring to become a member of the Club may be admitted on application to the Treasurer or Secretary, subject to the approval of the Committee at the next meeting.

21. Each member shall pay an entrance fee of 2s. 6d , and a quarterly subscription of 2s. 6d., to be paid in advance.

22. When the Funds of the Club amount to two pounds or upwards, the same shall be deposited in the Post Office Savings' Bank, or in some other Bank to be approved of by the Committee.

23. Each member shall have the name of his Club on his bicycle.

24. The Captain shall have command of all meetings for exercise, and on all excursions, and the route to be taken shall be decided by the majority of members going on the excursion. The Captain may at any of the times mentioned in this rule appoint a deputy.

25. Each member shall supply himself with a whistle, to be used only as signals as follows—one whistle, general muster, two to mount or dismount.

26. When four members or more are mounted they shall ride two abreast, and such a distance shall be kept as shall allow the right-hand man to fall to the rear of his left-hand man in case of single-file being necessary, and in all cases to obey the rule of the road.

27. A sum of money, not exceeding one-third of the annual revenue of the Club, shall be devoted to the purchase of prizes, to be competed for only by members of the Club.

28. No member shall be allowed to compete for any prize of the value of or exceeding £2 2s., except he has been a member for six months previous to the race at which the prize is to be contested for.

BICYCLE CLUB RACES

Rules for Competitors.

I. The races will be strictly confined to amateurs.

II. Any competitor entering in a false name will be disqualified.

III. The course will be —— times round to the mile, and the running will be with the right inside.

IV. Should a machine by accident be rendered unfit to compete the rider will be allowed to borrow and use another machine of equal merit, subject to the judge's approval.

V. All competitors must wear University or Club costume, and run in the colors they give on entry.

VI. Immediately preceding the commencement of each race, every competitor will receive from the clerk of the course a ticket bearing a number, corresponding with his number on the programme, which must be fastened on his right breast and worn there during the race.

VII. The time stated in the programme for each event will be adhered to as strictly as possible. A bell will be rung before each race, when the competitors are to answer to their names opposite the referee's chair. After the names have been called over a second time a start will be effected.

VIII. No competitor will be allowed to start except he wears a ticket with his proper number.

IX. The start will be effected by report of pistol.

X. No attendant will be allowed to accompany a competitor in any race.

XI. Any competitor starting before the signal, to be put back at the discretion of the starter; on a repetition of the offence, to be disqualified.

XII. Riders must pass each other on the outside, and be a clear length of the bicycle in front before taking the inside; the inside man must allow room for his competitor to pass. This rule will be strictly enforced.

XIII. In a race without using the handles, competitors must ride with arms folded or kept breast high; and any one touching the hands with his arms, hands, &c., will be disqualified.

XIV. The race for the —— cup is open to members of the —— Bicycle Club only, and shall be contested for consecutively at its race meetings, and shall become the absolute property of anyone winning it twice in succession, or three times in all. The winner each time to receive a handsome gold medal.

XV. The committee reserve the power of postponing the races in case of wet weather. On no account will entrance fees be returned, or expenses allowed to any competitor in case of postponement.

XVI. The referee's decision to be final.

XVII. The committee reserve the right of refusing any entry, and of disqualifying any competitor before he starts without giving their reason for so doing; and of making any alteration in the programme that may be deemed necessary.

XVIII. No Bicycles will be allowed to enter the course except those to be ridden in the races.

Entries must be sent to the Secretary on the forms supplied only, in time to be received by him not *later* than on ——————
All fees to be paid on entry, otherwise the entry will be void.

For tickets, forms of entry, &c., apply to the Hon. Sec.

Admission to the ground, —— Reserved Seats (in the Pavilion), ——. Carriages, ——.

HANDICAPPER.————————————   JUDGE,————————————

STARTER, ————————————   REFEREE,————————————

FORM OF ENTRY.

I hereby agree to abide by the above Rules of the —— Bicycle Club.

*Name (in full)*____

Address ____

*Please to insert my Name for Event No.*_____________________

*Club (if any)*____

*Colors*____

Diameter of Driving Wheel _________________________________

*Signature*____

FINIS.